—◇—

ADVENTURING WITH GRANDPA JONES

—◇—

H.B. Jones

TABLE OF CONTENTS

INTRODUCTION

These stories are not all of my adventures, only the ones not included in my previously published books: *True Tales of a Wyoming Generation*, H. Barnett Jones, *True Tales Slightly Skewed*, H. Barnett Jones. (For the remaining ones, I used H.B. Jones as the author):

Surviving The Old Folks Home, Dancing With Arthritis at Arthur Murray (why I started dance lessons at age 86) and *Memoirs of the Old Folks' Home in the Time of COVID and Trump*.

Also, if you're ever conflicted about religion, I suggest a book, which is a result of my years of research, titled *A Secular Analysis of the Bible, and Examination of Religion*.

This current book, *Adventuring With Grandpa Jones*, is suitable for general reading by anyone, but eventually I'm hoping that it will fall into the hands of my younger family members: children, grandchildren, nephews, nieces, and finally, my great-grandchildren and beyond.

My goal is for them to know how things were in the late twentieth and early twenty-first centuries; what we did, our problems, joys, beliefs, passions, achievements, foibles and failures.

I also want these offsprings to know me, who I was, even those who are just an idea for the future when the right time comes.

Dig in everybody, and enjoy my adventures; even the ones I didn't.

Grandpa Jones

PART ONE

OUTDOOR EXPLOITS
OF MY SIXTIES

Chapter 1
High Places

The year 1953, the ascent of Mt. Everest by Sir Edmund inspired me.

Four years later, I found myself in Mexico on the summit of the 17,887-foot volcano, Popocatépetl. After recovering from a brief wave of nausea from the altitude and the stench of the sulfuric fumes from the bowels of the mountain, I felt an indescribable euphoria as my eyes scanned the rest of the world below. This was the first bliss in a love affair with climbing mountains.

By the time I was in my sixties I had many peak bagging notches on my climbing belt.

To further demonstrate my passion, I am including this poem that I wrote, titled, "HIGH PLACES." Part of the credit goes to an essay by G. McNamee in *The Sierra Club Desert Reader,* which inspired me to write a poetic adaptation.

High places send humans to strange modes of being,

To states of fear, reverence and awe.

Believers connect these high points to the spirit world,
because mountains hold dominion over the land,
and gaze sternly down on their lowly subjects.

For some, heights arouse fear,
for others they inspire exhilaration,

but whatever mode they cause,
they change our being.

Mountain tops are the abodes of Deity,

where humans experience expanded depth,

and inner peace born of sensory sharpening,

not unlike a religious thump on the head.

While staying high up, our eyes become clearer,

our ears finely tuned,
our food more flavorful,

the music of bird calls richer.

If you choose to climb mountains,

or just view them from afar,
You must confess they still pull you,

as their peaks pierce the sky.

For me they are holy,
my spirit flies free,

I find in them refuge,
and peace there forever.

CHAPTER 2
A HIGHLY CHARGED HIKE
IN THE HIGH COUNTRY

After being pelted by rain and bombarded by near misses of lightning bolts, we lumbered into the parking lot where our car sat, stoically awaiting our return through the deluge.

We hastily tossed our packs into the back of the SUV and gratefully slid into the seats, taking special measures to avoid messing up the interior with our wet clothing. What a relief to finally escape the fierce elements!

Bob started the car, preparing to drive out from under the branches of a large pine tree, as that is not a safe place to be when a thunderstorm is still raging.

But right then, Rene, one of our hiking companions drove up beside us and rolled down his window. "Could you. . ." he started, and Bob cut him off. "I can't talk right now," he shouted impatiently, glancing up at the mammoth tree above us. This wasn't the time to worry about drawing maps just so Rene could go find that thrift store with all the cheap prices.

Earlier that morning I had ridden with friends Bob and Kim in their Mercury Mountaineer SUV. At the Mt. Tallac trailhead just west of Lake Tahoe, we met Rene, from Nevada City, and Ed, from Reno, to climb to the summit.

Before starting our trek, Bob had extolled the great bargains of a certain clothing discount store in Reno. Rene, always seeking to spend as few shekels as he could get by with, perked up his ears. "Now, exactly where is this place?" he inquired.

Bob gave some rudimentary directions but Rene persisted: "Could you draw out a map for me before we leave today?"

"Sure, no problem," Bob promised, and we started up the trail.

Mt. Tallac, rising above the southwest shore of Lake Tahoe, is the tallest mountain on the lake's immediate shoreline. After reaching the summit, we enjoyed the sun as we ate lunch. Some clouds were forming in the west, but that wasn't unusual, and we were too charged up with high Sierra euphoria to pay much attention to any stinkin' clouds. We had no clue about a much higher-voltage charge that we'd encounter later on.

We finally hauled our carcasses off the warm granite and headed down the trail. At Gilmore Lake, as the sun peeked through to highlight a beautiful array of wild flowers, I veered from the main trail onto a faint path.

"What are you doing?" Rene asked, his face wrinkled with concern.

"It's a neat shortcut," I explained. "It's not on the maps, but it is a real trail that was constructed years

7

ago and was formerly in use." We hiked for a few minutes in the forest and then came to the beginning of the lower part of the trail that had been blasted out across a very exposed talus slope through rocks and boulders.

The views were expansive, and we could see Lily Lake way down below, with little ant people moving around their tiny cars.

Then we heard the first ominous rumble of thunder. "Oh, great," Kim mumbled, and her face darkened as much as the thick clouds above. We felt the first rain drops and after a few minutes, the heavens opened their floodgates, which prompted a brief stop to throw on our waterproof jackets.

Then jagged lightning shafts, shooting out of the black sky, exploded like malicious cannon balls, warning us with split-second blinding brilliance. The thunder claps were scant seconds after the flash of lightning.

Each bolt shook the ground under our feet. I felt like I was leading my troops through a bombing range. There was no shelter, or relief, no place to take cover. All we could do was keep hustling down and leave our survival to fate. *Either we'll be struck down by lightning or we won't.* We scurried on down double-time and got to the bottom remarkably unscathed by the lightning gods, but wetter than a bunch of puppies who had fallen into a lake.

Despite the dingy mass of cloudiness above, I still had my dark glasses on. I'd been too busy dodging lightning strikes to even think about them.

My long cotton pants, great protection against the sun, brush and bugs, lapped up water like a lost mongrel at a desert oasis. I felt my trousers hanging heavier and longer.

And I wasn't the only one. Ed's pants were drooping too. At the car I said, "Bob, my pants are so wet I'm afraid that they'll soak your car seats. Is it okay if I take them off?"

"Yeah," he replied, "I think we're going to have to take ours off too." So we all started pulling our pants off. Bob and Kim were in the front seats and I was in the back.

The thunder was still booming, and the lightning kept crackling. Our atmosphere's ether was alive, still permeated with electric energy. So despite Rene's entreaties for a map, we escaped, albeit trouser-less, from the dangers of falling debris from the big tree.

As we were pulling out, Bob remarked, "I gotta make sure we don't have an accident. If they found us like this, they'd think we were a bunch of weirdos."

"Yeah," Kim joked, "and besides I don't have on my best underwear." Then she spoke to me in the back seat without turning around, "Barney, are you . . . out there . . . or what?"

"I've got my jacket draped modestly over my lap, don't worry," I said.

Rene had been following us, and soon started flashing his headlights. He was one persistent dude, and not happy with Bob's refusal to risk our lives with a bolt from heaven back at the tree. Bob finally pulled over and Rene came up beside us.

"I was just wondering if you could get me that map now," he asked.

"Well," Bob said, "I don't think so . . . I mean, we're sitting here in our underwear."

You could tell Rene was frustrated, but he just stammered, "Oh, uh, well, uh, okay then."

I was surprised he didn't ask about the "underwear" remark.

Both cars then continued to Highway 89 and turned in opposite directions.

Before we got to Albertson's parking lot where I had left my car, I managed to pull on my damp trousers. Didn't want to be arrested for indecent exposure when I got out, you know.

I told Bob they could just drop me off and go on home. "No," he said, "our bladders are about to burst, we gotta go to the restroom . . . *now!*"

We stopped at the traffic light, waiting to turn into the parking lot. I became aware of a violent shaking of the seat in front of me. I don't know how the hell he did it in the driver's seat, but Bob got his pants on.

"This is the only time I've been glad that it was a long light," he quipped.

We parked, and I went to my car as Bob and Kim waddled with gritted teeth to take advantage of McDonald's facilities.

We did hike this little used trail again on subsequent occasions, albeit under blue skies. But for us, it is now known as: *The Lightning Trail.* I don't know if Rene ever got his blessed map to find the super discount store, and frankly, don't much care.

Chapter 3
The Rainbow Lodge Connection

PART ONE

A preface: When someone says that they ski, it usually means that they go to a resort, buy a ticket and get on a chair lift or aerial conveyance of some sort, have a nice ski down, then do it again—and again. That's what I call *yo-yo skiing.*

Nothing wrong with it, I did that too—sometimes. But what my companions and I preferred is what I think of as *real* skiing. It's called *Back Country Touring,* and we climb up the mountains, one ski after another, upward. It's lung power and muscles, baby!

"Well," a resort skier may say, "that sounds like a lot of work!"

But we don't see it that way. I've always said that climbing builds character, raises spirits, and keeps your head in the right place. We *earn* our turns.

When you reach the high point, the sense of accomplishment is strong. You survey the view below and give thanks. And you are soon to be rewarded, when you ski down through the mostly untracked snow.

You and your companions are out in the beautiful and serene lap of nature, not on a slope with a multitude of people. If the weather turns bad or the snow is crappy, that's part of the adventure. You learn how to deal with it.

So of course you have to know what you're doing. Avalanche awareness and instruction is important. You must know the routes, know where you are and have all the necessary equipment. There are some trails, but you usually don't follow them if you already know the terrain or how to use a GPS device.

For making turns on all kinds of snow, from fantastic to lousy, many of us use the Norwegian technique called the telemark turn. We have cable bindings which allow us to raise the heels alternately for turns.

But some of our ski buddies, who yearned to be free from the crowds and expense of resort skiing, have recast themselves to the back country mode. All they had to do was make a slight adjustment on their ski binding to *free the heel* so they could climb. Then for the downhill, they locked the heel down for their parallel turns. This is called *Alpine Touring, or AT.* Many of our ski excursions are mixed, with both AT and telemark skiers.

Our favorite outings were peak climbs, but we also toured, going over high ridges, dropping down, continuing on across varied terrain, and go on to another high point that we have a hankering to explore.

This is the kind of topography we negotiated in this following story, "The Rainbow Lodge Connection."

—◇—

We did not intentionally go out to test our mettle in a raging blizzard. We hoped to have calm skies and perfect snow, but we must be prepared for anything. Neither did we stay indoors just because of a forecast of "Partially cloudy with possible snow showers." So when we place ourselves into the unpredictable hands of the natural world, some days it can give us mortals a sucker punch. And this was one of those days.

We started our ski tour from the parking area off the I-80 freeway and headed north toward the inviting beyond. The sky was partially cloudy and the temperature moderate. We crossed over the Castle Peak Ridge and started down toward a little cabin named the Peter Grubb Hut. Our daylight faded, the clouds darkened like the face of an angry ogre. And the wind slapped at us with malevolent gusts. It was time for a lunch break, so we sought refuge inside the hut. It was pleasant therein, but by the time we came out, a full-blown blizzard greeted us. The flakes were piling up and the visibility was limited.

"Where's Castle Peak?" Randy asked. "I can't even see it."

"It's right about there," said our leader, Dave, as he gestured upward, "but it's all socked in. We'd better start back."

So we cut the tour short. No exploration of the *Great Beyond* today. We stepped into our skis and hunched on our packs to start the trek back to the cars. We made a line of Gore-Tex jackets, each keeping sight of the person ahead.

When we crossed over the ridge, we could tell that the visibility was worsening with each ski stride. Anytime we looked up, the wind blasted our faces with snowfall. We stuck together and followed Dave, who was flying blind himself.

Although this was before high tech devices like the GPS, we used the compass, and we knew that if we kept heading south we'd eventually come to the I-80 freeway.

We slogged along, slowly but steadily. Then I heard a voice behind me yelling, "Marilyn stopped, we'd better wait for her to catch up."

Kristina and I went back to wait for Marilyn. "Okay," I murmured, "I see her . . . she's coming." Then she stopped . . . adjusting her pack, or glasses or something.

"Oh, c'mon Marilyn!" Kristina sounded uncharacteristically impatient. "Well, I mean, we don't want to be here all day!"

"Oh, well," I said, "This will give us a longer trip, more bang for our buck." Despite the conditions, I was disappointed that our outing was ending so soon. Besides, the fresh snow was great for attempting fancy turns—and adventurous when you could hardly see what you're doing!

But soon Marilyn caught up and after a while we were close enough to hear the traffic on the freeway. "Well, here we are," Dave said, as we stood at the edge of the highway, "but it's not where we left our cars."

In the blizzard conditions we had unknowingly veered off into a different drainage that led us too far west. But we weren't stranded, because Rainbow Lodge was right across the highway.

We left our skis on the front deck of the lodge and stepped into the restaurant, one after another, craning our necks to see if there were any unoccupied tables. The buzz of chatter diminished suddenly, and eyes turned to this line of strange white humanoids entering their cozy, warm domain. I suppose we looked like apparitions, covered with snow, especially if we still had our parka hoods up, seeing only frosty faces and a few frozen mustaches. And that was just the women. The men looked even worse.

But all kidding aside, I doubt that anyone could tell the women from the men. Then we found some tables and removed our snow laden winter garments, and finally resembled humans again.

After warming up and sipping some hot beverages, we had to face the issue of how we were going to get back to our cars. The answer was obvious. Bruce and I volunteered to step out onto the highway to hitchhike to Boreal where the cars were. But lacking the confidence that either of us would attract the attention of any driver, we persuaded Kristina to come out and stand in front of us as bait, playing the part of the helpless but alluring female in distress.

That did it! A car with a couple of guys stopped and rolled down a window, yelling, "Need a ride, honey?"

Kristina walked up to them and said, "Yes, thank you so much! My friends here need a ride up the road a ways to get their cars."

The two guys then noticed us, hesitated, and grunted, "Aw right, get in."

A while later, we were all contentedly on the way back to the lackluster, snow-free flatlands after another Sierra Adventure.

Life is good sometimes.

PART TWO—THREE YEARS LATER

It was obvious that it was not going to be a *bluebird* day. The wind, calm a few minutes ago, started gusting. The sky was blotchy with unreadable clouds.

The snow was as wet as my breakfast corn flakes after I pour milk on them. Would it turn to rain? Skiers want rain as much as teenagers want parental advice.

Should we cancel? Our leader, "Hug" (short for Huggins), was game to go. "But it's up to you guys," he said.

"Well," John said, "we came all the way up here to ski, so I say, let's ski!"

"Heck, yeah," agreed Terry, and the rest nodded in agreement.

Besides Hug, this hardy crew included Barney, that's me, Mary, Randy, and John and Terry. The final destination was The Rainbow Lodge, but in a roundabout way. This was a few years after the trip when we got off course in the blizzard and ended up at the lodge by accident.

This time Rainbow was the intended destination. And it wasn't in blizzard conditions. However, neither was it a marvelous weather day.

First we did a car shuttle, leaving a car at the Rainbow Lodge but starting our tour at Troy Road, a location a few miles a way. (We like to do *loop trips* with no backtracking, all new scenery along the way.)

"Okay," said leader Hug, "our first high point will be Matrimony Ridge." This was the moniker we hung onto this high ridge because a couple of our ski companions got married there.

From the ridge we veered to the north at the Royal Gorge Cross County Resort sign which we called the Rainbow cutoff. We weren't alone. We ran across many other fresh tracks in the snow. But they were all made by critters, from squirrel to coyote size. We were the only humans to venture out on this soupy day. What were we, intrepid or inane?

The snow coming down turned wetter. Our waterproof Gore-Tex jackets were shedding water rather than snow flakes. We became aware that the clouds had lowered and visibility was marginal, so route-finding was a challenge. But this time, leader Hug used his trusty GPS and kept us on the right course.

After a while, our hunger pangs motivated us to look for a suitable place to sit and munch lunch. The snow gods then rewarded our forbearance of the sloppy conditions. We came upon a little-used Royal Gorge warming hut for cross country skiers. How nice to enjoy a leisurely, warm and dry shelter for lunch! We *almost* felt like we were being wimps for seeking such luxury. But the nourishment and rest gave us renewed energy and enthusiasm for inserting ourselves into the clammy ambience to ski some more.

We set out and came to a spot that Hug called "the drop." It was the best downhill portion of the day! Maybe a bit intimidating for some, but mostly fun and exciting.

Soon we cut loose with a bunch of whoops and hollers, making nice S tracks in the wet snow. Not as good as dry powder, but still fun, and we left only a couple of sitzmarks (depressions made by butt marks).

Our "drop" took us down to the level of old Highway 40. Soon we caught the aroma of Irish coffee and we knew that we'd hit our target.

We entered the Rainbow Lodge, attracting no attention. The sloppy conditions had dampened our garments, but not our spirits.

I look over at a bunch of folks at the bar who were watching a football game, with their big butts flopped over the stools. They stared blankly at the screen until they gave out a whelp when their team scored.

Other patrons were eating, drinking and chatting happily at the tables. They had been warm, and dry, and physically inert all afternoon. I pitied them for they knew no better.

I was so grateful for my day outdoors, with our bodies in motion, while breathing life-giving air as the breeze peppered us with wet snow flakes, accentuating how alive we were.

Later, at home, the well-deserved hot shower caressed me more than ever. A cool beer was more special and my self-made dinner tasted better than usual.

Afterwards, I stretched out lazily on my recliner to read. I earned this. But thank goodness it wasn't how I spent the entire day.

CHAPTER 4

AN IRASCIBLE THUNDER BOWL

I'd been confronted before by self-flushing toilets, but none like this robotic, hyperactive bad boy.

With just one look at this gray ugly bucket, the words *military* and *spartan* came to mind.

The first thing I noticed is that the usual seat that you raise or lower is missing. What's left is what you sit on.

Well, I've had it worse. For example, outhouses at rural residences of Wyoming, or just squatting in the woods and hoping that the leaf you wiped your bum with wasn't poison oak.

Nonetheless, I was not ready for what happened that first night at the VA Blind Rehab Center. I was sitting innocently on the above-mentioned facility when it suddenly roared to life. Although I wasn't moving physically or otherwise, this crazy commode started flushing noisily and furiously, and I sensed its hostility. *What does it have against me? Doesn't it realize I'm just doing what it was built for?*

And it wouldn't stop. It made such a racket there in the middle of the dead, quiet night; like the sound of a rocket launcher, followed by a cascading Niagara Falls. I could feel the wild churning below me as it sprayed up against my exposed hindquarters.

Then I heard some knocking. *God, I wonder if it's the guy in the adjoining unit knocking on my wall, furious about the ongoing clamor.* I finished what I was doing as quickly as nature allowed, and eventually the flushing ceased.

The next afternoon when I had to make use of the thunder bowl again, the wild churning action repeated itself, as did the knocking. This time I thought it was one of the nurses knocking at my bedroom door. I yelled in irritation, "I can't come to the door now!" *Why do they always come just when I'm in the bathroom?*

Eventually I figured out that the knocking was a result of the water rushing through the plumbing. It was the pipes that were knocking! I was stuck with a devil toilet.

But then—serendipity! The big guy next door was uncomfortable in his small bed. My bed was bigger and he asked if we could trade rooms. Since I'm such a nice, pleasant person, I readily agreed.

After the switch, I visited my new toilet. It looked the same, but seemed to have a more benign aura. And indeed it was calm and efficient, not a vengeful demon like the other.

The guy I traded with seemed to be happy too. He said nothing about a rogue toilet, and I wasn't about to ask him! If it liked him better than me, fine!! But I can't imagine why the heck that drab, ceramic crapper had it in for me!

CHAPTER 5
THE FORMIDABLE DANA COULOIR

First of all—*couloir*—what's that? The word is French, pronounced *cool-war.* But gargle the final R a little if you want to say it like you're French. (But don't choke on it.) It means corridor or passage. Our anglicized pronunciation comes out sounding like *cool-ar.*

It's a common mountaineering term, and when we say it, we're talking about a steep chute. We use the word with respect and a bit of trepidation, especially if we're about to ski one.

On that pristine May morning in Yosemite National Park, I had no thought of skiing any stinkin' couloir. This was just one of my solo ski tours. Sure, I prefer going with friends, but when no one else is up for a promising trip, going alone, using extra caution, is better than sitting around wishing I was out frolicking in the natural world.

My goal this day was to ski to the summit of Mt. Dana, a 13,061-foot peak just inside the Yosemite Park entrance. The bright morning was crisp with blue skies, early sun and frigid temps, but promised a pleasant spring day. Mount Dana loomed proud and white, boasting complete snow coverage from summit to base.

As soon as I started my ascent, I realized this pristine white surface was frozen as hard as a boiler plate. Even with my skins on, my skis didn't grip the snow firmly like they usually do.

Skins are a brilliant technological innovation designed for climbing mountains on skis. They have a permanent adhesive on one side that you stick to the ski bottom, and a one directional mohair on the other side which slides forward but not back. Unless you're trying to climb on frozen, glassy terrain as I was attempting to do that morning.

I struggled up to a semi-level shelf where a couple of other skiers had stopped to rest and reconsider. This is when I first met Chris and Martha. They were friendly and conversant, so we chatted a bit during this brief respite.

Chris then told me, "We've decided to put on our crampons." He was right. If you've heard of crampons, you may know these spiked devices are usually used on boots for snow and ice climbing. But they do make them for skis as well, and fortunately I had a pair in my pack. The days are rare when we need them, but this was one of those days.

With our crampons holding us securely on the icy escarpment, the three of us started out again, chatting as we went.

As we got higher, the wind buffeted us, and eventually Chris and Martha got ahead and I lost sight of them. Later, however, I saw them on a different route, but we were all heading toward Mount Dana's summit.

When I reached the top I felt the usual euphoria I always get when I finish a climb. I sighed with pleasure and drank in the spellbinding vistas from my frozen *thirteener*. To the east I could make out another world of crags and canyons. Looking on the other side far below me, Lake Mono glistened with sun sparkles.

"Hey Barney," I heard someone call, breaking my reverie. It was Chris. "Come on over here and have lunch with us." That sounded good. A leisurely lunch in a little shelter with my new friends. The sun not only blessed us with warmth, it also performed its essential task of softening the unfriendly, solid top layer of rock-snow that we'd been skiing on. We looked forward to that magical metamorphosis to friendly *corn snow* for our descent.

We finally stirred ourselves to crawl out of our nest. We put our skins and crampons all snug in our packs and our lunches in our bellies, giving us renewed vigor.

As we discussed possible routes down, Chris said, "Why don't you come with us? We're going to do a loop and that way you don't have to backtrack." That sounded enticing. I'm a sucker for loop routes with all new scenery.

"Well, okay," I said, "if you can lead the way."

Gratefully feeling the sun's rays favoring us mortal humans, we started out again. Soon we were heading up a hill.

"So, we're going up more?" I asked. I thought our climb was over.

"Only to this last high point," Chris answered, "then we head down."

"Oh . . . you mean the . . . couloir?"

"Yeah, after we get over this hill."

When we reached the top of the high point we stopped and looked down, sizing up the plunge we were about to take. I could feel my heart beating faster and it wasn't from the altitude.

As we stood there, our three sets of skis lined up, I couldn't help but notice how my equipment contrasted with that of Chris and Martha. My unsophisticated telemark skis compared poorly with their hotshot alpine touring skis which were wide and sturdy. Their bindings had been loosened at the heel for climbing, but for the downhill they locked the heels down solid to make their aggressive turns.

Their solid shiny plastic boots reflected a colorful hue from the sun's rays.

In contrast, my scuffed, black leather Asolo boots looked like a poor relative of the ski boot family. And my battered telemark skis with their cable binding surely didn't belong to any downhill ski aristocracy. They were also skinnier and longer that downhill skis.

But you ski with what you have, and I was a telemark skier and proud of it. The telemark technique is Norwegian, named after Telemark, Norway. (And please don't confuse it with its antithesis, teleMARKET). This technique was invented to increase skiing efficiency in all kinds of ungroomed snow, be it breakable crust or messy slop.

My humble telemark skis did have metal edges and I respected both them and my cable bindings. In order to make a turn, we telemarkers need to raise up our heels alternately to slide one ski forward for the turn. We call this *free heel skiing* and have a favorite saying: *Free the heel and your mind will follow.*

Okay, we had reached the moment of truth—the proverbial point of no return. It was too late to back out—I was committed.

To get to the top of the actual couloir, we first had to ski down a very steep pitch from the high point where we had stopped momentarily. This served as an initiation or warning for what was in store for us.

At the top of that gigantic bowl, we paused once more. I was awestruck. *My god, it looks like a mile of vertical snow!* Probably a typical first timer's impression. I don't know the exact degree of incline, probably between 35 and 45 degrees. But by any standards, impressively precipitous.

Chris shoved off, followed by Martha. I hesitated for a moment, feeling like a hapless new military recruit on his first mission. They dropped into the bowl at an angle to keep their speed in check. Chris and Martha did a series of turns and were gone.

I stood there and pondered: How do I negotiate a turn when it's this steep without ending up with my skis heading downward in a runaway mode? This was in my early days of skiing before I learned the telemark jump turn where you do most of the turn in the air. What you most want to avoid is losing an edge and falling. In a couloir, it's not a matter of just falling and then getting up and continuing from there. Your motion is downward when you fall, and when you hit the surface of a slope this steep, you don't stop there. Instead you accelerate downward like a chunk of avalanche debris.

I knew a technique adjustment was necessary.

I decided to try what I called a modified *tele stem turn*. As you initiate the turn you pick up your uphill ski, angle it toward the direction you want to turn, then aggressively bring the other ski parallel to it across the slope. This has to be done with quick movements. It's easier to describe than to perform. But it worked! I skied a little farther down using this technique and saw Chris and Martha standing, a ways off to my left.

"Everything okay?" I shouted.

"Sure," Chris answered, "we're just getting some photos of each other on the Dana glacier." Well, they are sure laid-back, I thought. Here they are skiing the formidable Dana couloir and they're acting like tourists.

But I wasn't into touristing this day so I continued my careful descent. In due time, the three of us reunited at the bottom. It was nice to relax a bit and luxuriate with the benevolent spring rays caressing us. We all shared the wonderful rapture that ski adventures like this inspire.

Finally we got into our skis once more and navigated around a half frozen lake to get back to our starting point. Chris and Martha graciously invited me to have dinner with them that evening, but I reluctantly declined because I needed to finish my drive home before it got dark. Yeah, I could climb a 13,000-foot peak, but was afraid to drive at night.

(Many years later, living in an old folks' home, I was reminded that any guy who could drive at night was automatically the darling of the ladies. But, by then, I couldn't even drive in the daytime—Ha! Life is interesting—if you don't weaken.)

During the following years I skied the Dana Couloir several more times. By then I had plastic boots and wider, shorter skis, very similar to current downhill resort skis. But I was still a telemarker, using free-heel gear with cable bindings. I had perfected my tele jump turn, so instead of feeling the intimidation of that virgin trip, I appreciated and respected the magnitude of this gigantic bowl, a glacial cirque that I was allowed to visit, and felt minuscule by comparison.

On one of those visits, I was having a pre-couloir lunch on the summit with some other skiers that were hanging out there. They appeared to be part of an organized group. One man, evidently their leader and mentor, was giving advice and also regaling them with some of his many adventurous ski excursions. His exploits sounded impressive and his followers listened with fascinated attention.

After a while they all got up and prepared to head for the couloir. After a short delay, I also slipped my pack on, snapped my cable bindings firm, and set off in the same direction.

By the time I dropped into the couloir, most of those skiers were quite a ways ahead of me, making their way down. I then became aware of a solo skier to my right. He was carefully side stepping, skis horizontally across the slope, taking one cautious step after another, down the couloir. It was the leader of that same group I'd been with at lunch. *What in the world is he doing?* I thought. *He must be waiting for one of his acolytes.* But I saw nobody, just him. He didn't seem to be in distress, just very intent on his side stepping down, so I just waved and continued tele-hopping down the couloir.

At the bottom, as usual, we skiers enjoyed a rest stop, and traded tales of the day's experience. After a while I saw that the sidestepping leader had made it down. He came over to join his group. "I'm sorry," I heard him say to one of the girls, "I just froze up there, and that's all I could do."

I don't think he was a coward. I believe that a long, steep chute of snow and ice can impose a powerful effect on anybody, anytime. And none of us knows how we will react until we are facing that exact situation.

The cirque on the backside of Mt. Dana. The couloir is the narrow strip at the top right of the photo.

Chapter 6
Climbing the
Cascade Volcanos

MOUNT HOOD, OREGON

Until recently, I had not known the scope of the feat I had accomplished—and how lucky I had been. But when I researched Mount Hood for this writing I came across testimonials about this "scary mountain," and saw some hairy videos of Mt. Hood climbs that reminded me of Mount Everest expeditions, even if on a lower scale.

It was June of 1993, I was 64, and I had a couple of northwest peaks in my sights.

"Mount Hood, huh?" one of my mountaineer friends grunted. "Yeah, I tried twice and had to abort both times."

I knew Mount Hood was the highest mountain in Oregon at 11,240 feet in elevation. But it was a popular climb and I wondered why it was so rife with difficulties.

"Why did you have to abort?" I asked my friend.

"One time bad weather, the other time danger of ice and rock fall."

I found a brochure from the Mt. Hood Forest service:

Mt. Hood is a technical climb for experienced mountaineers only. You should start your climb by about midnight at Wy'East Day Lodge at Timberline. Climb up under the stars and you should reach the summit when the sun is rising. By about eight o'clock you should be off the summit face and down as far as the Hogsback. [a wind-carved ridge of snow]

Be advised that rescue operations are complex and may take a long time, as it is a remote area.

Yeah, I'd heard about that starting-at-midnight bit of advice.

But climbing alone in the dark was a deal breaker for me, so I looked for an alternative. First I checked the weather. The forecast predicted clear, calm conditions, and moderate temperatures, with no storms in sight. Ideal!

I knew there was a ski resort at Timberline Lodge with a chairlift that was open into early summer, for skiing on the lower part of the Mount Hood glacier. If I rode the chairlift up, I could quickly ascend the first 2,500 feet of the 5,000-vertical-foot climb. That's half the way to the top! I reasoned that the steep terrain of the summit block is the only dangerous pitch on a storm-free day. If I saw that the conditions were bad, I could just go down and make use of my lift ticket for the rest of the day.

So that Friday morning at 8:00 a.m. I was first in line for the chair lift and got on the chair with two other folks. I was wearing my backpack and it forced me to sit too far forward on the front half of the chair. I had to hold on tight to keep from sliding off into thin air. But I made it to the top of the lift without scooting off my precarious perch, and once on the snow-covered terra firma, slapped my climbing skins on to my skis. It was all uphill from then on, under my own power.

When I got to the base of the summit block, it appeared that a climber was about half way up the steep face. I could detect no evidence of any avalanche conditions or debris.

At the very bottom of this steep pitch was a large *bergshrund* (a deep and broad crevasse). With its massive jaws wide open, it seemed to be waiting to devour a hapless snow boarder or anyone else plummeting downward like a hockey puck. There was no way I was going to ski this upper part. I ditched my skis and strapped my crampons on to my hard, plastic ski boots. Ski poles in hand, I started my careful ascent. I don't remember it as being too hard or hairy. (Or maybe I was temporarily insane and the fright wiped out my memory of that portion). The surface was in good condition, soft enough to get a good foot grip, but not sloppy.

When I reached the top, I was too consumed with summit ecstasy to worry about the imposing gradient going back down. The open-jawed *bergshrund* would still waiting to eat me alive.

But after evading that big gap, I could look forward to a long, enjoyable cruise down this huge mountain that had permitted me to encroach upon its territory.

I encountered several other summiters, and some conversation ensued. They evidently had been waiting for the snow to soften before climbing down. As my eyes were surveying the horizon and several snowcapped peaks, a guy said to me, "You're lucky you did the climb now. When I came up it was hard as a rock!"

Timing is crucial in our daily lives. And this day my timing was impeccable.

MOUNT ST. HELENS WASHINGTON

On May 18, 1980, a violent eruption blew off the beautiful symmetrical cone of Mount St. Helens. This explosion removed the upper 1,300 feet of the summit. The total destruction of the area was regrettable, as was the loss of life, like Harry Truman, the old codger who refused to evacuate his home at Spirit Lake.

To a much lesser degree, this eruption was regrettable to me as well, because the summit of Mount St. Helens, which no longer existed, was on my list of Northwest peaks to bag. So I had to do the next best thing: climb to the rim.

On that sunny March day of 1994, the mountain was white, with a new covering of a foot of new snow. This would be another ski ascent. It was going to be a warm day, so I got an early start. At first it looked like I had it all to myself, but then I saw a figure up ahead, so I hustled to catch up with him. That was lucky, because he said he had climbed this mountain the day before and knew the best way to go when covered by a blanket of snow. It was called the *Worm*

Flow Route because it had been formed by old lava flows that had created a series of curvy ridges.

As we chatted, I learned that this guy had climbed Mount St. Helens forty-three times. "That's how I spend my weekends," he told me. I reflected on this. As much as I like peak climbing, this character needed to *get a life!* He wasn't skiing, just booting up without crampons, as the new layer of snow wasn't hard.

It had been easy so far, then we came to some pitches that were so steep I had to carry my skis and walk. My companion expressed skepticism about the wisdom of doing his on skis. *Well,* I thought, *just wait until we go down, then I'll be sailing past you, hooting with glee!*

Despite the steep terrain, it was stable, without any avalanche danger. Soon, the incline was less steep and I put my skis back on. As we kept slogging up, I thought I could see the top. *But no, that's probably a false summit.* Every time I've climbed a mountain, I thought I had spotted the summit. *Almost there,* I would think. But as I approached, another summit appeared—then another.

But this mountain had no false summits, or any summit at all. What I saw was the crater rim itself, and suddenly here we were on it. The once proud peak, 9,600 feet in elevation, was no more.

It occurred to me how easy it would have been, in poor visibility, to take that next step and walk right over the rim and down into the abyss.

On this clear day the views were magnificent: I could see the lava dome that had formed down in the crater. Spirit lake glistened far below us, and in the distance Mount Rainier jutted up prominently. As always, I gave thanks for another mountain high, even though a summit was lacking.

Now for the fun part: skiing down! My skeptical companion would find out now why I was on skis instead of tramping down like him. But I'm the one who had to *eat crow* because I had not taken into account the Mashed Potatoes. That was the name we had for the snow in this condition. It was like trying to make turns in someone's freshly poured patio. This kind of snow is also called "Sierra Cement" in our California mountains, and "Cascade Concrete" in the northwest. I worked hard to get down without breaking an ankle. My companion reached the bottom way before me.

But that was okay. It had been another adventure, and I had gone as high as anyone can go on Mount St. Helens. It was a different experience, and the views were stupendous. I now had another notch of a well-known mountain in my climbing belt. I wouldn't have missed this for anything.

CHAPTER 7

TREKKING IN THE ANDES

SUMMER, 1995

MY AGE, 65

It was cold. I had three pairs of wool socks on, thermal underwear, wool pants, a wool shirt, a down jacket, a wool cap and gloves. And I was in my sleeping bag.

This was my second Peruvian excursion, having finished the first one a few days prior: the famed Inca Trail to the mystical Machu Picchu. (Described in *True Tales of a Wyoming Generation*, Chapter 48, "Summer Travels"). There had been about a dozen clients and three guides to get us to this symbol of the Incan Empire, built around 1450 AD.

But on this second trip, there were only two clients, Sarah and me. Sarah was a thirty-five year-old medical doctor. She was also on the Machu Picchu trip, and some of the other hikers and guides found her disagreeable at times. They also told me that Sarah was somewhat unhappy that her next hiking partner was a sixty-five-year-old dude. She was afraid that I would be too slow.

After all, it was to be a multi-day trip, and was billed as "extra strenuous."

This expedition would take us way back into the isolated Andes mountains where there was no civilization. Our route circumambulated the glaciated Mount Auzangate, whose icy summit reached to 20,905 feet. To complete this circle we'd have to climb up into some pretty thin air.

"What's it going to be like out there?" we asked the guides before the trek.

"Beautiful, remote," they said, "and COLD." It was winter south of the equator, and though sunny during daytime with reasonable temperatures in the fifties or sixties, at night the mercury drops some thirty or more degrees. We stayed snuggled in our bags until the sun hit our tents. Then began the process of removing one by one all those layers. Soon we would hear footsteps by our tent, and would unzip to find a little pan of warm water for washing, and hot tea. I don't drink tea in the morning, I drink coffee. But I drank this tea. Afterward we would go to the dining tent for breakfast—with coffee.

Besides Sarah and me, our crew consisted of our head guide, the cook, and two horse wranglers for the two horses that carried our duffels and all the other equipment. All Sarah and I had to carry was our day packs. When we got to each night's camp site, our duffels were there in front of our tents, already pitched. I thought of it as luxury camping.

Our meals were pretty good, considering the circumstances.

The guides brought some of the food, bartered from the natives in the early stages of the trek when in the lower farming areas. They also took some beautiful big trout from the clear, rushing streams.

Every evening during dinner, our cook would boil big pots of water and pour some of it into our personal water bottles. They were hot when we took them to our tents to retire, so besides drinking water, they served as foot warmers in our sleeping bags at night.

They kept encouraging us to "stay hydrated" as we gained elevation on each day's journey. "Sarah, you're not drinking your tea," the guide kept saying during supper.

"No," she replied a bit defensively. "I don't want to have to get up and go out . . . "

And neither did I. But I drank my tea anyway, because I had secreted a pee bottle in my tent. Even so, it was a challenge getting through all those layers when I had to use it.

To pull off this Auzangate circuit, we had to acclimatize, not only to the low nocturnal temperatures, but even more, to the high altitudes. It helped that we had spent some time in Cuzco, which sits up at 11,500 feet. And when we got going again, every day's trek got us gradually to the next step in our altitude staircase.

Before we reached the highest passes we leveled out on a plateau at about a 13,000-foot elevation where we stayed for a few days. It was very remote there. No towns, no electricity, no lights, no roads, no motors—and no people. The terrain looked bare of human existence—or so we thought.

But after we got tents pitched and started to settle in, human visitors appeared—fathers, mothers and children. Where did they come from? We looked towards the direction from which they had materialized and saw their camouflaged hovels, made of the same material and color of this piece of the earth they inhabited.

They crept up, wide eyed, so obviously intrigued. We were their entertainment, their TV, foreign objects of curiosity. We couldn't talk to them because they spoke no Spanish. They are *Quechuas,* and the lingo they speak is *Quechua,* the original language of the Inca Empire.

We were such an oddity to them that they sometimes crowded in, staring at our green tents and white, creamy sun-blocked faces. Our dark glasses must have given them the impression of big glassy eyes.

I said they spoke no Spanish, but evidently they'd had some contact with other excursions, because some of the kids knew how to say *"Dame dulces."* (Give me candy.)

Our guide had brought some pencils and paper instead. That's better than rotten teeth, since these indigenous youngsters had no dental care.

Some of these inquisitive kids were walking around, peering into our tents. This troubled Sarah. "What if they peek into my tent while I'm undressing?" she complained.

I'm afraid I wasn't very supportive. "If they want to see me naked," I responded, "that's their problem, not mine."

In the morning as we broke camp, a few *Quechua* souls appeared like ghosts. A last farewell? Or just more idle curiosity? Their clothing was light and shabby. I glanced down at their bare toes protruding from their *yanquis* (Peruvian sandals).

I wiggled my own toes, trying to warm them up inside of my two wool socks and heavy leather boots.

I stood there in my wool pants and cap, sweater and Gore-Tex jacket, waiting for the sun to heat up to a balmy fifty-five degrees. Soon we resumed our trek, and the movement helped pulse the blood to feet and hands.

Since we were completely removed from city illumination, or any kind of artificial light, the stars were dazzling; they shimmered so brilliantly we felt like we could almost reach up and touch them. These meridional heavens offered us a personal viewing, and we had front row seats! Our guide, an amateur astronomer, pointed out all the important stars and constellations. This was the first and only time for me to see the Southern Cross, a gift presented by the southern hemisphere.

The following day we would experience the highest altitude of the trip, which would test our conditioning. Although it wasn't the icy summit, we nonetheless prepared to climb over the first of the Big A's 15,500 foot passes. Were we acclimated and ready to confront the rigors that Mount Auzangate had in store for us? Only one way to find out: one step after another, upward.

And that's what we did—maybe not easily, but successfully. We were able to climb to such heights only because our ascent over the past few days had been gradual. I was surprised and pleased that I felt just fine going over the top.

Sarah did fine too, but she was a ways behind me with the sweep, and had to take more breaks. And she was a bit chagrined because her sexagenarian trekking partner had scrambled across the top of the mountain more easily than she.

Back on level ground we had a respite, and that's when we met up with another troupe of English-speaking trekkers. But they didn't sound like us! More like, "Hey, mate, what are ye doin' out heah, got no better sense than us, hah!"

Yeah. Aussies. And though they fit their role as hearty Australians—rowdy, irreverent and undaunted—they were good blokes, friendly and jovial.

We heard about a so-called warm bathing hole created by natural hot spring in this area, which served as a kind of hot tub. After going bathless for several days, it was irresistible. The Aussies jumped right in. I slipped in too, but later learned what a colossal mistake it was. Here's a heads up, fellow trekkers: If you want to enjoy a primitive warm springs bath with other people, *keep your head out of the water!* That night and for a few days later I had a pesky head cold.

The next issue was whether to eat a dead sheep or not. Some local character was roasting a sheep in a crude underground oven. I guess it was something like an Andean Luau, and he had invited all the trekkers on site to partake in the eating of this special mutton feast. But after just being duped into immersing myself in a-germ-laden hot tub with some unbridled Australians, I was reluctant. However, our guide said it would be an insult to the Peruvian host to refuse. Sarah was afraid too, but had a good excuse because she was a vegetarian. So I lied that I was a vegetarian as well, and got a pass.

The Aussies had no such qualms. "I'm nevah one to pass up free grub!" And so they went and scarfed it down. But I wanted to avoid scarfing, then barfing— on top of the world. Because the following day we were going to cross the second high-altitude pass.

Up and ready the next morning to traverse the other 15.5K pass of King Auzangate, I was relieved to see that my head cold didn't impede my progress upward. I chatted with the cook who was leading the pack. Sarah was behind with our guide, struggling a little, but moving along steadily.

By late afternoon we were settled in our new campsite. It was different from the others, because we were closer than ever before to the imposing, glaciated giant whose terrain we had just intruded upon for the second time. His Majesty only barely tolerated our intrusion, grudgingly allowing us to trespass.

This was the coldest night of the trip, and also the noisiest. For *HE* was alive and kept reminding us of his presence and power with ice falls and other angry rumblings.

This one night, instead of retiring to our tents right after supper, the guides built a big bonfire, using animal dung as fuel. We sat hunched around the flame, engaged in conversation, with periods of silence, becoming aware that this Andean caper was soon coming to an end.

That night, in our cozy cocoons, we were frequently awakened by crashing and growling, as large segments of ice, rock and dirt broke apart. We weren't the only living beings here, just the most insignificant. Nonetheless, we were grateful for the short span when we were a part of this exotic world.

Could you go through something like this and not be changed? I have oft revisited this indelible slice of my life and reminisce about exploits of the distant past. Such a fortunate guy am I.

CHAPTER 8

REFLECTIONS

Our ascension this day was not one of those hairy escapades, but it most certainly was one of the most memorable.

Our goal was to reach the summit of Echo Peak, located between Lake Tahoe and Desolation Wilderness. There was no trail, so our route led us up a craggy ridge. It was fun scrambling up the solid granite, choosing a solid handhold and stretching for the next handy foothold.

On the summit we relaxed, had lunch, and enjoyed the high tranquility. The views gave us a profound exhilaration. On the western horizon, the austere, gray granitic Crystal Ranch thrust its jagged outline up into the contrasting azure of the cloudless sky. To the east, the huge expanse of Lake Tahoe sparkled in varied tones of emerald and inky blue.

Down below us . . . Echo Lake shimmered in the sunlight. We five humans, recognizing our insignificance, fell into an appreciative silence. The sun reflected from countless, tiny ripples on the surface of Echo Lake. As we gazed down, we were mesmerized by the twinkling of the infinite reflections which produced a fixed pattern across the entire lake.

A small motor boat started up and slowly churned from one end of the lake to deliver passengers to the other shore. The motor noise was muted at our elevation, so our ambience remained tranquil. As the boat's bow plowed leisurely through the uniform, sunscaped surface, we watched it form a "V" across the little existing twinkle patterns, growing wider each few seconds. It only took the boat a few minutes to traverse the mile and a half length of the lake.

By that time, the configuration of the lake surface had undergone a gradual but absolute metamorphosis. The "V" spread out like two elongating wings, extending to the rear, stopping only when they lapped against the shores and licked the sandy beaches and rocks. Simultaneously, small waves bounced from lake center to edge, erasing the previous twinkle pattern that had been so dominant. Because the lake surface was so alive with reflection, a graphic example of cause and effect was displayed. In the time it took me to eat an apple, one innocuous boat crossing had transformed the entire lake surface.

Then a bothersome thought intruded into my carefree consciousness. This benign spectacle was meant to be a reminder: Most of what we humans do in our mechanized, high-tech society—from the trivial to the grand—is changing the natural world that nourishes us.

CHAPTER 9
SKIING MOUNT SHASTA

JULY 1997

After the frigid winds and sleet that King Shasta punched us with last year, I swore we wouldn't attempt another ski ascent to the summit until the region was sizzling in the middle of a heat wave. On Friday, July 17, 1997, it was—and we did.

I was in my post retirement *heyday* decade, the super sixties. I felt like I could master the summit of any mere fourteener I encountered. I was unstoppable—for a sexagenarian. But big mountains are not so easily impressed.

My faithful companion, Ken Condriva, from Livermore, CA, whose reasoning powers were evidently as flawed as mine, was hot to make another attempt to reach the top of Mt. Shasta on skis. What a great experience it would be—and then the exciting ride down, a board on each foot!

So there we were again at Bunny Flat, the 6900-foot elevation parking area. We hit the trail at a dawning 5:20 a.m. We were able to put our skis on just a few steps up from where we parked our cars.

From there, we skied up to about the 10,000-foot elevation, just below Lake Helen. That was the easiest part of the climb. At that point we had to tackle the headwall of Avalanche Gulch and the Red Banks, which were more like chutes than a walkable incline; too steep to climb up on skis.

So we strapped crampons on our boots, and secured the skis to our packs. This additional weight was immediately noticeable.

By this time the sun had just peeked over to this side of the mountain, but the snow had barely started to soften. To advance upward in the mostly frozen snow, we had to kick step up. That meant that on this abrupt angle, we had to kick in the front point of the crampon, brace, balance and push up to find a placement for our next step. Sometimes the snow was so icy and firm it took a hard kick to establish a solid foothold. Later, as it warmed, there were spots where the snow was too mushy and our footing caved in.

We had to keep our heads down to see where to kick that boot. After a while I was compelled to look up to check our progress. What progress? The top didn't appear to be any closer than it did the last time I looked. Despite our efforts, it was as though we had been standing still.

Though disheartened, we fought our way up on that snowy treadmill to nowhere. *Sure, I like a challenge,* I thought, *but I want to enjoy it. Is this fun?*

We stopped just long enough for a gulp of water and a snack. And also to pump ourselves up a bit. *Yeah, we can do this!*

Finally we found ourselves closer to the top of the Red Banks, at a higher location than we had expected. We realized then that we had come on a different route than usual, having climbed straight up over the banks in a continuous ascent.

And we felt it. I heard Ken say, "My body doesn't want to go another step!" I agreed, and was also on the verge of flopping down to rest, but it was too steep to have a comfortable rest stop, so we forged on longer than we wanted until we came to some more forgiving terrain.

After some rest and nourishment we felt revived, and continued on. We were on the bottom half of *Misery Hill,* the last significant ascent before the summit block. Encouraged with new energy and optimism, and continued on.

Then a sharp pain hit my right leg. I tried to ignore it, then to work it out. But then, like a second adversary offering reinforcement against the enemy, my left leg cramped as well. After sitting for a few minutes, I tried again, but it was like walking on two pain-ravaged, wooden two-by-fours. We were so close—out of the nearly 7,000 vertical feet we had climbed, now there were only about 600 more to go!

But I was toast. I hated to be this close to the top and not finish the climb! But I had to make sure I would be able to ski back down this monster mountain. I needed to give my legs a good rest.

"I can't go on," I told Ken. "I'll wait for you here." I could tell he was concerned."Well . . . okay," he said, ". . . but I hope when I look back, I'll see you coming."

"Me too, but. . ."

I had already hiked to this summit four times, just not on skis. Ken had never been to the top. This was his chance, and what the heck, he was just a young 49-year-old, he could do it!

Wearing my Gore-Tex jacket and hood, I was comfortable in the sun's high altitude rays and occasional light wind gusts. I looked out at the rest of California, far out and way below. The folks down there were sweltering in the 106-degree temps. Then I became aware of an airplane flying below me here in my snowy nest.

I started thinking about our descent. Though I wouldn't be starting from the summit, I would still be able to do the almost all of Shasta's downhill. We had planned to ski down the West Face rather than Avalanche Gulch, and I was higher right here than the entry to that nice sloping western exposure.

My reverie was then interrupted by a voice: "Hi, you doin' okay? Your buddy on the top said to check with you on our way down to see if you needed anything."

"No, I'm fine. I took a couple of Tylenols because I had some big-time cramps. But thanks for checking."

After a while I heard some skis and there was Ken. "So you made it, good for you!" He was happy and told me he had to hold his arm way out to take a picture of himself, his first time on this 14,180-foot summit. (Ken had done what nowadays we call a Selfie, with our smart phones.)

"Okay, well, it's getting late," I said, "Let's see if I can ski down this monstrosity." I wondered if my legs were going to work well enough to get me down this mega-mount.

First we had to find the top of the West Face. We had talked to a couple of snow-boarders earlier who knew the way, so we followed their tracks until we found ourselves at the right place to start our descent.

"Let's do it!" Ken said with a gleeful smile. With his Alpine Touring gear he took off in a series of smooth parallel turns. I wasn't far behind, keeping up with my telemark technique and whooping, "YEE HAW!" *Now I'm having fun!*

The snow on the upper part was perfect, but got a little soft lower down. When we got lower, we crossed over the ridge to come out right below Avalanche Gulch. Then we took the same route we had ascended that morning and followed a finger of snow almost to the car.

My downhill skiing muscles are obviously better conditioned than my ice climbing muscles. But they got me up high, and more importantly back down without cramping.

I did not conquer Shasta. But neither did Ken. Climbers only get to the top if the Mountain permits it. It can be unyielding when it wants—even malevolent. We must never fail to give our mountains respect.

I'm happy to have had this experience, and glad to say I skied the West Face of Mt. Shasta. However, I doubt if Shasta will have any more chances to beat up-old Grandpa Jones.

73

But this weekend excursion story is not finished. I'm not done with this multi-day escapade. The next day I'd confront a less intimidating mountain, by the name of Lassen Peak.

CHAPTER 10
LEISURING AT LASSEN

The next morning after our Shasta exploit, I had to leave Ken at the campground outside of Shasta City with his old ailing car. He hoped to fix the problem soon and get it going. I had to leave because of a commitment to meet my friend Blair at the Lassen Peak parking lot. It was imperative that I be there because I had his skis in my car. He had left them for repair in Tahoe City and I'd picked them up for him before I left for Mt. Shasta. I hoped Ken would have his car repaired and catch up with us there too. Friends Terry and John also were going see us there and be with us for the Lassen climb.

To Blair's great relief, I arrived at the lot about the appointed time with his skis. John and Terry were waiting there too, so we were all ready and eager to start the climb.

It was another warm, beautiful day in the high country, and by the time the four of us started up the trail to Lassen's summit, it was 11:00 a.m.

I worried that I might not make it to the top due to residual Shasta spasms of expended leg muscles. However, my recuperative powers must've been good, because my climbing mechanism was functioning well. Indeed, it seemed so easy after Mt. Shasta. And, unlike Shasta, there is actually a hiking trail to the summit, which was mostly snow free. Even though it's a steady climb, those 2000 vertical feet, compared to Shasta, seemed like ambling along a placid path through a meadow. Surprisingly, the extra weight of the skis in my pack wasn't as onerous as usual.

We took a long time on top to relax, munch a lunch, feel grateful, and pity the folks below, who merely had driven to the parking lot and spent their time there gawking upward.

As we were making preparations for our descent, I noticed another climber who had just arrived at the summit. It was Ken! Clever mechanic that he is, he repaired his car and got here just in time to ski down with us.

When Terry and John got a good look at the sharp angle from the top, they decided to walk down a ways where it wasn't so intimidating, and enjoy skiing down from there. But Blair, Ken and I eyed the slope with keen anticipation. A few sun cups (melted depressions in the snow) and rivulets littered otherwise smooth snow, but we were able to avoid most of them and had a nice ski down. As usual Ken glided easily with his smooth and efficient alpine turns, while Blair and I executed our fancy tele-turns. We released our jubilation verbally with a couple of YA-HOS. *This is just us, folks, enjoying life. You should try it sometime.*

We rounded the shoulder of the summit ridge and stayed high to ski the steep face that looks right down on the parking lot and its cluster of onlookers

This was to be the last run. Not only of that day, but for Blair, the last one this *season*. So we wanted to do it right. Ken went first, from right below us. Then Blair and I went, negotiating our finest tele-jump turns on the smooth, steep snow surface. When we got to the parking lot, the ranger there told us we had provided entertainment for all the tourists there, who evidently had watched our every move.

Blair had to go home, but the rest of us spent that night at a campground just outside of Lassen Park.

The next day I guided Ken, Terry and John on a ski tour into Bumpass Hell Hot Springs, one of my favorite Lassen ski jaunts. We walked around on the boardwalks, fascinated with the bubbly, steamy boiling pools and sulphuric smells. We had it all to ourselves, without the congestion of tourists, since the summer hiking trail was still blocked with snow.

By mid-afternoon we were back at the parking lot, and braced ourselves to come back to the hot flatlands. Though not eager to return, we were thankful for the high-country respite from the obscene summer sizzle. What a great snow year it was!

[JUST FOR THE RECORD]

Obviously, the snow year of 1997 was outstanding. But several years after, there was one even more unforgettable:

The air was crisp and our skis slid softly toward Castle Pass in the fresh powder. It was a typical winter day for January. **But**—*it was not January. It was October 29, of 2004: The earliest ski season we had ever experienced.*

This storm dumped three feet of snow, and in following days, the storms kept coming, laying down layer after layer of the pristine white winter coat.

This glorious phenomenon allowed us to ski through mid August if we were willing to go where the snow was still hanging on. And we were willing.

Little did we know that the winter of 2023 would reap a record snowfall, beating the 2004 record. But this time I could only enjoy it vicariously through my younger, dear friend Blair who was living in Truckee and still skied the back country.

CHAPTER 11
THE BIKE HIKE FROM HELL

On a warm summer day
My family came out to bike

Cruising nice trails that they like
But the route was ugly with very little to like

By Barney Jones, on site patriarch

"Do you have any extra water?" Jordan asks. "I'm parched, and Brock needs a drink too."

"No, sorry," I answered, "I didn't bring much and it's gone. I need some water too."

I seldom get so thirsty, but on this day, the sun was scorching and the trail was punishing. Sweat exuded in rivulets. Making it up to this upper ridge crest had been debilitating. We were above the tree line, so there were no trees to provide shade.

How did such smart people get in such a pickle? This trip had been a bust so far, and I was the instigator. I, the patriarch with all his wisdom found the route for this family mountain bike outing. I even scouted it out and rode the first part of it. What was I thinking?!

There were seven of us: my son Brian, his partner Lance, my other son, Jordan and his boy, Brock, grandson Dustin, and me, the injudicious instigator.

Our trip started out benignly, on Highway 89 south of Truckee, sailing smoothly along on the asphalt. But what the hey, we're mountain bikers, so then we turned off onto a dirt road. That led to a dusty single track and we started gaining altitude. Fine. But then it steepened, and the surface became a bike-hostile bed of jumbled rocks, some as big as cantaloups. I saw dismay on the faces of my dear family members that read: *What the hell?!*

So what do you do when the trail isn't ridable? Going back wasn't an option for this group, so we dismounted and started pushing our bikes upward. The sounds of shoes and tires crunching across the rocky path broke the majestic mountain tranquility, mixed only with some grunts, grumbles and muffled curses.

However, we finally got through the rocky muddle and pedaled up to the crest just below a peak called *Tinker's Knob.* As I gazed up at the summit not far above us, I had to acknowledge that today's target area would serve better as a winter ski tour, not a summer mountain bike expedition.

I looked around at my biking companions. The usual lighthearted banter was missing. We caught a little breeze up this high, but perspiration still glistened on our faces. We munched our lunch and stared down at the expansive views in silence.

Then, as Brock looked down at the rocky mess we came up, he mumbled, "I'm glad we got that over with!!" We all nodded in appreciative agreement.

This was a *loop trip* so we would do no backtracking. From here it was a decent trail, downhill all the way! It was what these young bloods had been waiting for. They love plunging down the trail on their specialized conveyances, and they're good at it. But I'm not. I have a T-shirt with an image of a mountain bike and rider tilted at a steep angle. The big letters above it read FEAR! It fits me perfectly.

We got our stuff together and everyone took off—except Jordan, Brock and me. They were adjusting equipment, so I started down. I was a bit hesitant and nervous, but made it okay on the first little descent, and stopped to take a look at the next challenge below me, while I waited for Jordan and Brock. Then I heard someone yelling in frustration above me, "THIS SUCKS!" It was Jordan, who had expected to catch up with me sooner, and thought he was on the wrong trail. After he wheeled up beside me, I assured him that they were on the right trail, and that the others were ahead. That brought big grins, and Brock hooted, "Yay, all down hill from now on!" and they took off, leaving only dust and joyful echoes.

That was okay. It was better to be back there by myself, not worrying about keeping up with the young hot shots. I proceeded downward, tense and attentive. No heroics, just survival; finish the day without breaking an arm or bashing my head in a dramatic OTH (over the handlebars).

It actually was getting to be fun. In a couple of places that looked too squirrelly for anyone but the best riders, I got off and walked.

At last the terrain leveled out. *All right, I made it down, no crashes, no gashes!* The dirt road was smooth and I took a big breath and started to relax, as I pedaled easily along.

I later learned that the rest of the crew had arrived at a suitable spot to stop and take a break and wait for grandpa. "He should be here by now," Jordan said. They waited some more. Then Brian decided he'd better go back to check on me, so he left the others and started back.

When he finally spotted me, I was off the bike, rolling it up a hill—in the wrong direction—heading back up the mountain!

"Dad" Brian yelled, "no, back this way!" So I turned around and came back down to him. He stared at me, his face manifesting confusion and concern. "Wow. Are you okay?"

"I crashed," I admitted. "Flew over the handlebars. I fell really hard and just lay there for a couple of minutes, feeling a little light headed. I think maybe I hit my head when I fell."

"What's my name?" Brian asked.

"Brian."

"Where are we?"

"On a mountain bike ride. I guess I got disoriented from the crash. I was wondering why it was uphill again. I had been cruising easily on the flat, but there was a rock in the middle of the road. I didn't see it because it was in a shadow. I hit it head on."

We rode on down and met the rest of the gang, and after relating my misadventure, we went on to Donner Lake Park Museum where we had left our cars. Our big loop started and finished there. We loaded up the bikes, then made a bee line to the nearest convenience store to assuage our unbearable thirsts.

I parked at the 7-Eleven and saw Jordan and Brock get out of their car, so I walked over to join them. Jordan turned away from me, his jaw set in annoyance.

"Hey, Jord!" I yelled.

Jordan pivoted around to face me. "Oh, my gosh, Dad; I thought you were some homeless guy coming over to hit me up for a handout. I didn't even recognize you!"

We all went in and looked for soft drinks, juice, pop, anything cold and wet. I took a bottle of Snapple out of the cooler and got in the cashier's line. I greedily gulped down the cold beverage even before I reached the cashier. Two teenaged girls were in the line ahead of me. One of them turned her head to glance back at me, then quickly turned back, and whispered to her friend. They moved as far away from me as they could.

Wow, I wondered if I stank. Then I remembered Jordan's reaction and pondered: My old shirt was sweat soaked. I had put sunblock on my face and rolled in the dust when I got knocked off the bike. My hair was undoubtedly disheveled and dirt was sticking to my sweaty clothes. I was tired, so probably had a hangdog look. Yeah, I must look like a homeless bum all right.

—◇—

That evening we all gathered for supper in my Truckee rental home. Brian was in the kitchen working on dinner, and I was beside him, helping. I bent down to get a pan out of the bottom shelf, and stood up too quickly. My head spun and the next thing I knew, I was on the floor. I had fainted, but Brian half caught me to break my fall. As I remember, I regained consciousness almost immediately.

I suppose I was exhausted and probably dehydrated. This was the only time I know of that I had symptoms of dehydration. And this had been one of the few occasions when I got so thirsty that I drank all the water I was carrying.

That day, I managed to scare the crap out of my family when they heard about the crash, and again when I fainted. But I also gave them a trip that would trigger vivid memories of one of our wild and unforgettable family outings.

However—there were no requests for another one.

Chapter 12
Skiing In the Rain

(WE WERE NOT SINGING)

JANUARY 17, 1999

The Rain in Spain falls mostly on . . . the INSANE (everyone else is undercover.)

[This ditty is to be read aloud with a cockney accent. I don't know why.]

When perchance I ski in the rain
For some stupid reason it addles me brain
I get this strange urge a ditty to write

And I can't seem to resist, try as I might

I arose to go ski this fine winter morn,
But looked out the window at a drippy wet storm,
But I was not frettin,' even though it was rainin'
'Cause up high it was snow
So I wasn't complainin'

Well, just short of Donner, I was almost to the pass
Did the snow change to rain?
You bet your sweet _____
(I couldn't think of a word that rhymed with pass)

My friends were all there a' preparing their gear
To go ski in the rain, now ain't that a bit queer?
We slogged up the ridge, my fingers were numb
We were squishy and sloppy this really was dumb!

So we went down to the hut
Peter Grub, where it's dry
Though skiing down in concrete made us wish we
could fly
But inside it was cozy, a fire in the stove
We got rather comfy and cheerful by Jove!

We finally came home with spirits renewed

And an attitude of gratitude weather be screwed!
I even did turns in that heavy wet snow
The Sierra cement no longer a foe

I suppose you can call me certifiably insane
Lackin' the sense to stay out of the rain
So please feel totally and charitably free
To rebuke me a little or just scoff with glee.

Chapter 13
How To Win Two Medals In One Race

MARCH 24, 2000

Every year my skiing cohorts and I looked forward to *The Kirkwood Cross Country Race.* It was special to us because this 20k course (12 miles) was an authentic *back country* race, with groomed trails only for the last part of the race. The first half of the race had a 1300-foot climb to cross the Sierra crest. For that we'd need climbing skins, just like one of our wilderness tours. Only after crossing the high point was there a groomed trail that took us to the *Kirkwood Cross Country Center.*

The smart thing to do is to save one's energy the day before such a demanding contest. But my noble intent to do so was weakened by a magical dump of fresh, white flakes that grabbed my eyes on arising Friday morning—the day before the race. It was a beautiful winter scene that beckoned to me like a beautiful bride in all her virginal white attire. How could I refuse her?

To avoid trail breaking in the deep powder of back country, we opted to go to the Sugar Bowl downhill resort, ride the lifts and save energy that way.

Oh, my, those days were so sweet. Some resorts at that time let a seventy-year-old graybeard ski gratis. All I had to do was go find the sign that said, *OLD FARTS SKI FREE.*

Yeah, big race tomorrow or not, I'm going to rejoice today in the thrill of the downhill!

And so I had way too much fun playing before race day. My lift ticket was free, but my seventy-year-old knees were not free of arthritis, and they reminded me that I was no longer that jaunty sixty-year-old who thought he was unstoppable. But, what the heck, my union with the sweet snow virgin surely was worth some slight discomfort.

(Here is what I wrote in my log, in order to record the day for posterity.)

It is now Saturday morning, March 24, and I wake up, drowsy, with a wisp of some exotic dream I can't quite recall. Probably something to do with snow virgins. And that brought me back to reality. *Holy cow, I'm doing a twelve-mile race this very day!* But after my date with the Snow Queen yesterday . . . maybe I'll just dog it, what the heck? They don't even have an age seventy division for the medals, only up to sixty plus. I'll be competing against a whole gaggle of perky sixty-year-old hotshots. My back country experience is no match for their specialized racing skills. I just do these races for kicks.

The top place winners have names like Sven and Bjørn, and I suspect they grew up in the old country, involved in Nordic skiing before they could walk.

So here I am, Saturday morning, milling around with the other racers, waiting for the start. Should I skin up now, or just before the big climb? If I have them on now, I'll be slower on the level part. But if I wait until later, I'll have to stop, take skis off to get the skins on, causing a delay. I opt to skin up now and move up to the starting line.

I see the top guns, Sven and Bjørn, poised at the front edge of the racers. Then— BANG! The starting gun turns the mob loose, and Sven and Bjørn leap out in front. Other racers, vying for a good position in close quarters, get their ski tips tangled up with each other, some even falling and tripping up others. Such is often the scene at the beginning of a race, with a bunch of adrenalin-charged competitors.

Me, I hang back, shuffling along on my skins, in the clear. After a while I get to the shelf right before the summit ridge, where most of the racers have their skis off so they can slap those skins on and start the climb. To my surprise, Bjørn and Sven don't have their skis on yet. Aha, a chance to get ahead of the front runners! I breeze by, delighted with my decision to put skins on before the start. I am ahead momentarily, but expect the Scandinavians to pass me at any minute.

But they don't. Why? Then it comes to me: skins and climbing is not their strength; it is mine. I hustle on and get over the crest, whip my skins off, and do my best to launch into the skating technique, racing style. Man, I'm really cruising! Then a blur swishes past me and all I can see in is Bjørn's back end—disappearing rapidly. Not that I recognize his back side, but it has to be him. No wonder the Norwegians always win the most medals in the Winter Olympics!

Then Sven whizzes by me, making me feel like I'm standing still. His movements are so smooth it looks effortless.

With optimism fading, I keep plugging on, pushing a little, but not overtaxing myself.

After finally crossing the finish line, I see Bjørn and Sven scarfing down the free goodies, and chatting casually. They have obviously been here for quite some time.

Most of the race results are already posted, so I wander over and check it out. I find my name near the bottom. Third place in the sixty plus division! How could that be? I came in forty minutes after Bjørn and Sven. What happened to all those other sixty-year-old hotshots?

In the medal ceremony, they always start with the youngest divisions, so I was the last to be called for my third place metal. Although I was happy to win a place at all, I was still a bit ticked off. I wanted some action taken to rectify this prejudicial assumption that anyone over seventy was too frail to make an effort in such a competition.

As the young lady placed the bronze medal ribbon around my neck, I said, "Thank you, but I'm seventy years old, and . . ."

"Hey, everybody," she interrupted, "Barney here is seventy years old!" The crowd obediently cheered and she turned her back and ignored me. Through her thin T-shirt I saw her brassiere strap. *If I snapped that, I bet I could get her attention!* But that would be counterproductive, as well as rude, so I just touched her arm.

"So I wondered," I said, "why you don't have a seventy plus division?"

"Oh . . . right," she said, then reached into a box. "Here you go, your gold metal for seventy plus!"

And that, boys and girls, is how you win two medals for one race.

CHAPTER 14
THE TETON TRAVERSE

APRIL 11 & 12, 2000

The ad in my ski magazine caught my eye immediately:

RENDEZ VOUS SKI TOURS
Glen Vitucci, owner and guide

SKI ACROSS THE TETON RANGE
Experience a two-day back country adventure with knowledgeable mountain guides and overnight in a warm yurt.
This classic Teton tour starts in Victor, Idaho, and terminates at the Jackson Hole Ski Resort in

*Wyoming. The total distance is a bit over 21 miles
with 5300 feet to climb.
Rated by Outside Magazine as one of the "25 Trips
of a Lifetime."*

I've got to do this, I thought. This was 1998. In fact,
a couple of weeks later this mindset put me on a
windblown slab of slanted ice, listening to Glen
saying, "Not good conditions, but since you drove so
far I thought you might want to ski a few turns before
you head back."

That's right, I drove 805 miles to find out that the
weather had turned so bad we couldn't even think
about doing the Teton Traverse. So much for 1998.

The following winter I had company: my good friend
Blair and his lady friend, Deb. The weather was good,
and we were already up at Glen's yurt, waiting
excitedly to get started in the morning to complete
the trip to Jackson Hole.

But early the next morning we heard the unwelcome sound of high wind. Then we noticed little intruding snow drifts beside out bunks. It was a raging blizzard and a general whiteout. We looked at Glen. "Not a chance," he said. When the visibility was tolerable we headed back down the mountain. And home. My second Teton failure.

Blair & me. We didn't get this far that day

But we had not given up. The following year we arranged to stay longer by renting Glen's nice guest house for a whole week. That way we could wait for the best two weather days for the excursion.

This time we had two more skiers: Doug, Blair's friend, and my friend Ed. Doug's wife and two young sons were there as a support team as well as Lois, my friend from Denver.

Outside of the guest house.

The magic days were April 11 and 12 of 2000. I was seventy that year, and as fit as I had ever been. Blair and Doug were in their late thirties, and Ed was sixty-four. Blair didn't have the right skis and had to use rentals and Doug was mainly a down hill resort skier and not too comfortable with telemark turns, but his skill level was so high that he was undaunted.

Fox Creek Bridge.

On Tuesday morning we crossed the Fox Creek bridge just a quarter of a mile above our lodging and we were on our way. Including Diane, Glen's assistant, there were six of us.

We climbed the 2200 vertical feet up to the yurt, and had time to hone up our skills in the California-like corn snow.

The yurt was located by some great ski slopes and the ski conditions were good. We thought we looked good on this *Ego snow,* but watching Glen and Diane executing their turns so fluidly and gracefully, both telemark and parallel, kept us appropriately humble. Doug, an expert alpine skier, had mediocre tele gear, but did well in both telemark technique as well as parallel.

The four of us and Glen.

Blair was bombing down through the wooded area in good form, which was remarkable because a few weeks previous his doctor had told him that there was a zero percent chance of him doing anything like the Teton Traverse.

My friend Ed, from Reno, whom I called the Undaunted Iron Man, blasted downhill with his smooth tele turns in a low, stable stance.

I just had fun trying to do my tele hops in front of Glen's video camera, but he never seemed to be filming when I was hopping.

The yurt.

Early Wednesday morning—we heard the wind blowing. Diane came in from outside and said there were clouds forming in the west, from whence the storms usually come.

Inside the yurt.

Was this going to be a *déjà vu?*

"Are we going anyway?" Blair asked.

"We're going," Glen replied. By the time we got out and on our skis, it didn't look so bad. The sun was just coming up over the east horizon. "Go ahead," Glen said, staying back to take a photo of us, "just head for the sun."

Ed was already a quarter mile ahead and the rest of us on the way. "YEE-HAW," Blair and I exulted, "We're finally doing it!" All we could hear was the noisy squeaking of our skins as they slid over the frozen, bulletproof snow.

Starting on the way to Housetop Mountain.

To get over the Teton Crest we would have to climb up and over the top of a high point called Housetop Mountain, as it resembles the roof of a large house.

The climb wasn't bad except for the steeper pitches that were still frozen. That's when I learned the hard way that if your skins don't cover the full width of your skis, they're next to worthless on icy conditions. Then you have to depend solely on your

111

metal edges, digging them in as you side step up. Fortunately this difficult stretch was short. Later in the day these narrow skins would be a cause of much greater concern.

We made this first climb of the day, 1,700 vertical feet, in fairly good time, and by about 9:30 a.m. we were standing on Housetop Mountain, awed by the spectacles around us, including the sharp images of the highest peaks of the Teton mountains.

On top of Housetop Mountain.

After Housetop Mountain the route then angled down a sharp, narrow ridge with a sheer cliff on our left. Glen then asked us to walk down, carrying our skis. After all that uphill, then to have to take our skis off for the first downhill was a bitter pill. But we complied, not only out of respect for our guide, but also acknowledging that a missed turn or fall could result in disaster.

Doug, however, surreptitiously hung back, then skied down the entire ridge. Glen, instead of the admonishment we expected, just gave Doug a sideways look, probably relieved that he hadn't disappeared over the side.

The lower part of the ridge was gentler, so we put our skis back on to make it to the bottom. At one point, Ed fell and was sliding slowly toward the drop off. "No, not that way, Ed," Glen joked, as it was nearly flat and Ed easily stopped his momentum. Diane couldn't help but tease Ed a little, telling him she was sure glad we didn't have to call for an emergency evacuation today.

After completing what I now call Drop Off Ridge, we stopped for lunch in a sunny, sheltered nest of rocks, and after eating we were treated to a nice long descent in a wide bowl. The snow was a mite too soft, but very doable, and a heck of a lot better than boilerplate ice, anytime.

From that friendly, soft terrain in the big bowl, we then faced some unusual terrain: First, two miles of flats, after which we had to skin up again to climb 1400 feet to get over another high ridge. Glen pointed out the route, adding that some parts of it were going to be "ugly." Wow, was he right! We had to traverse up a steep, north facing mountainside on snow as hard as the bulletproof snow we started on that morning. Yes, solid ice.

Glen, Doug, and Ed got ahead of me because my skis started slipping on the steep, icy pitch. As before, my skins weren't gripping because they didn't cover the entire base of my skis. "Gotta get some wider skins," I growled. When you have to rely solely on your sharp metal edges to get a purchase, you have to kick each ski aggressively in sideways to the hill and then labor diagonally upward. That was not only tiring, it over-stressed my uphill knee and hip.

Even worse were the kick turns. As we climbed in an upward slant we came to the edge, so we had to reverse directions; back and forth across the slope until we reached the top.

A kick turn puts you in the most vulnerable position of all. Starting from what you hope is a stable standing position, you lift one leg and plunk that ski down so that now you and **one** ski are facing the other way—which means your ski tips are now pointing in two opposite directions. Your body is posed unnaturally, kind of like a beginning ballet dancer doing a complicated maneuver for the first time. Next you have to balance on the other leg and bring the second ski around, placing it parallel to the first ski. If things go right, you and both skis are facing the new direction. If not, you may be zooming down the hill like a hockey puck.

Blair, Diane and I finally made it to a level bench where the rest of them had been waiting and studying the route ahead. It looked like more ugly pitches. Should we take off our skis and walk it? I wondered. No, trying to kick steps in that rock hard snow would be even more precarious.

So, depending on our metal ski edges we started out again and discovered that it wasn't as bad as the previous pitch.

After a while we found ourselves above a huge bowl with a cornice on the top edge, and looking across at some rocky cliffs with near vertical snow chutes. Diane explained that extreme skiers like to ski those chutes. She told us that one day she watched one skier there who had gone half way down and seemed to be trapped there by a rocky outcrop; and that he stood there just gazing at those rocks, seemingly studying how big a jump it would be to get over the rocks and on down. I don't remember her saying whether he made it or not. Maybe he's still there. And maybe that's why I'm not an extreme skier. To avoid starting our descent right below the cornice, an unstable bank of snow, we took our skis off and walked around it. Then with skis on again, we side slipped across some soft snow and crust and around some rocks until we came to the open slope. That's when the real fun began. It was south facing which meant the sun had spared us from dealing with any more ice. I remember it was quite steep, but that didn't bother any of us, and we carved a bunch of nice S's as we enjoyed hot doggin' it down the mountain.

Jubilation and the jagged Teton peaks.

After one more little climb of 200 feet, we looked down from the top of the famous Jackson Hole Ski Resort. We had it all to ourselves because they had

117

closed for the season. Now we had 3,000 vertical feet to ski down. My heart and soul loved it—but my septuagenarian legs eventually started bitching loooudly. They were rubberizing, you know, jelly-like—I mean tired, man!

Not really surprising though, since we had skied a rather rugged 17 miles and a lot of up and down this second day. And according to Glen, these legs of mine were the oldest legs he knew of that had ever done this entire traverse.

So then there we were in Teton Village. We made it! We had left the yurt at 7:15 a.m. and arrived here at 2:45 p.m. Pretty good time. Yee Haw!

My friend Lois and Glen's wife Chris weren't due to shuttle us back until 4:00 p.m., so that gave us an hour to enjoy some celebratory beers in the interim. The village was almost deserted, but a convenience store nearby was open so we occupied a picnic table and hefted a few cold ones. It was a nice reward after a fantastic back country ski excursion.

POWDER MANIA

Thursday, some of our group went skiing over at the Grand Targhee Resort in Wyoming, but I was content to give my legs a rest. Blair, Lois and I went over to Teton National Park and took pleasure walks as we gazed up at the towering peaks of the Tetons.

For Friday we had no exciting expectations, but the Rocky Mountain weather had a surprise for us. As we began to budge from our bunks, we heard the phone ring in Ed's room. A moment later Ed came in and announced, "Glen said they had six inches of fresh powder at the Grand Targhee."

"*Fresh powder,*" once spoken, had an electrifying effect on every skier in the building (which was everybody but Lois). We switched into double time and mobilized. It reminded me of war movies where the sergeant yells, "Front and center in ten minutes, ready for combat!"

Lois graciously offered to fix some eggs for us before we left and we uttered a few grunts of approval as we scurried around gathering up our gear. Blair suggested she scramble them as it would be faster. But the eggs were poached and it was the people who were scrambling to get to the freshly powdered mountain.

After a short time five adults and two young boys filed out and piled into their cars, leaving Lois to marvel at the pandemonium that the word *powder* had on these seemingly normal people.

CHAPTER 15
BORN TOO SOON

MY JOURNAL ENTRY FOR JULY 9, 2006

Sometimes I wonder if I was born too soon. Today, when I hiked to the summit of Castle Peak, I was greeted by four girls. Young women, I suppose I should say, but to a guy in his mid seventies they're all just girls.

They were so vibrant and friendly, out climbing a peak without any need of boy friends to lead the way. It was a beautiful, sunny morning and these gals were dressed accordingly: lots of skin exposure, skimpy tank tops and radiant smiles.

Where were they when I was that age? In my generation girls were not only discouraged to do sports, they were not even allowed. I suppose it was considered "unladylike." But how nice it would have been to go out hiking with girl friends back in my youth.

They could be cheerleaders, but otherwise they were steered into the "feminine" pursuits, like sewing and cooking; you know, preparation for their role of wife and mother. Nothing wrong with that, except that it limits the female potential.

So it does my heart good to see girls out on their own, hiking, skiing, running, biking, or competing in various sports.

I wonder if boys nowadays realize how lucky they are to be able to have feminine companionship when out in nature enjoying their sporty pursuits.

This outlet can also divert some of those raging hormones for which young males are notorious. It can lead them to think of the opposite gender as friends, not just conquests.

I sat there with those lovely girls, exchanging tidbits of conversation. I was attired in my usual nerdy, sun protective mode, with long pants, long shirtsleeves, sun hat and a white, sun-blocked face. Such a contrast to them.

"I'm a melanoma survivor," I felt compelled to explain. "That's why I'm so covered up."

"Well, I'm sure not covered," said the tank-top chick. "I hope I'm not sorry some day." She glanced at her lightly bronzed arms and legs.

"I sure was," I replied, "I could have died if I hadn't caught that cancer early."

"Oh my goodness!"

"And it probably started when I was about your age," I continued.

"Ooh . . ." she murmured.

As I was eating my lunch, I enjoyed eavesdropping on the somewhat esoteric girl talk.

Finally they started stirring in preparation to leave. The pretty blond with the skimpiest tank top then turned to me. "You inspired me to be more careful," she said. Then she put on her shirt. *But the downside,* I thought, *is that she's covering up nature's art.*

"Oh, good for you," I offered, and waved goodbye as they disappeared over the rim of the summit.

On my way back down, I caught up with the gal who had put on her shirt earlier. She and one of her girl friends had stopped to chat with a couple of young dudes. She had taken her shirt off, and was posing for a photo—chest out, skin gleaming, silhouetted against the brilliant blue summer sky.

"Hey," I yelled, "You're all uncovered again."

"Well," she answered defensively, "I still want to . . . look my best . . . you know . . . at certain times."

I figured that the mating instinct was at work here. So much for the independent woman who doesn't need a man. You just can't fight nature!

Chapter 16
Jones Family Hikes

A BALLAD

Blessed be the Jones family hikes, because it means family together, active, and enjoying nature.

On a Jones family hike, don't expect to walk ten minutes then sit around and watch TV. But neither will you be subjected to a gung-ho killer pace.

These family outings are structured to favor the lowest common denominator; comfortable for grandparents, grandchildren, toddlers, babies, pregnant women, and all in between. Sometimes it's just a day hike, but occasionally we rent a big house in a nice setting.

Our first family hike, nearly thirty years ago was Steep Ravine Trail from Mount Tamalpais State Park. Despite the trail's name, it is a mostly a benign, downhill trail of two miles ending at Stinson Beach. There, we had lunch, and relaxed. Later the strongest hikers went back up, did a car shuttle, and collected everyone. Other venues included Lake Tahoe, Oregon, Tabletop Mountain out of Oroville, as well as other localities too numerous to remember.

However, kids have grown up, gone to college, gotten married, had kids of their own and moved away. So it is now more problematic to corral all these multiplied number of folks in one place at the same time.

Nonetheless, it is my fervent wish that this tradition will endure through the generations, long after I am gone.

The following is a collection of snippets that I offer so that my family member can recall some memories, and others can catch a notion of what these once-annual assemblies felt like.

—◇—

A rental, not one but two houses on the bluff overlooking the great Pacific. Friday night sees Chef Brian, famous for his five course meals, relegating to each helper, who will be proud later to own a part of the scrumptious repast.

A convivial ambience prevails with no shortage of wise-ass joking. Palaver abounds, wine flows, and the patriarch sits back with a smile, admiring his kin like an Italian godfather.

Munchkins, Amelia and Miranda, convert place mats to hats on heads, giggling. Adults observe with tolerance. Little ones tucked safely in bed allows mature ones to copy the place mat-on-head caper, giggling same as the munchkins.. Not to be over looked the old guy is spotted with a green mustache.

Morning dawns beautifully, calling for a stroll on the beach.

Invisible, devilish blasts of air smack us in the face, flatten hat brims against ears. Hope's breath is snatched away by gusts as are words we are trying to exchange. Give me a blizzard any day. Retreat! Sand blasted sandwiches! Back to base camp. Some suggest sheltered trails away from the beach.

Dinner! Good humor carried over, wind tunnel trauma be damned! Hugo's seafood pasta, salad and garlic bread. Pungent breath contest later. Patriarch gives usual rambling, disjointed grace, but doesn't fall asleep.

After supper, Munchkin merriment.

Amelia: "Why was the skeleton afraid to cross the road?"

"Because it had no guts!"

"Knock knock."
"Who's there?"
"Amelia."

"Amelia who?"

"Amelia JONES, DUH!" (pulls strands of hair. Shy smile.)

Next, slide show exposé. Today's Candid Camera of events revealing victims' *worst side.* Brian's witty, descriptive remarks. Merciless and funny as hell. Laughing till stomach hurts.

Ah, trouble in paradise? Giulia, arm in sling, Tim limping with sore ankle. But all make it like champs to Shell Beach, breathing in the sea air and vistas. Inspired, press on to Goat Rock. Oh no! Now they're toast. Fatigue. Stranded. A heroic rescue by Julie and Hope, chauffeuring them back to civilization. All happy, kick back.

Patriarch warns group of a sickness: watching TV instead of nature's splendor or chatting with loved ones.

Dusk. Playing tag with the ocean waves, running back and forth, back and forth, untiring, like a dog chasing balls. Look out, there's a big one, farther and faster. A stumble, a dive, and a roll. The old man escapes a dunking. Comical, caught it in the slide show.

Bonfire at the beach, walking home in fog, a ghostly specter stalking, threatening Lance and Dustin. "It's just me, guys," Jordan says.

Different night after another delectable-palate-pleasing repast with ample beverages. Playing around on the cliffs. Hey, did he take a tumble?
Jose Cuervo, you're no friend of mine!

Sunday night, some folks have left, no dinner plans. A seafood restaurant, classy, delicious—and expensive! Brian and Lance pick up the tab! Bachelors, with salaries but no dependents—yet.
Monday morning. Fooey! Time to check out. See ya next time.

Part Two

◊

Older and Back
In the Flatlands

Chapter 17

Back Surgery? Never!

It was April of 2009. The bar patrons were there at Bezel's Bistro and Booze in Truckee to drink and fraternize, but the captivating chords of a Spanish guitar exacted a pause in the chatter.

This was different! The rousing tones of the Flamenco reverberations could not be ignored.

Flamenco dancers came onto the floor, spinning, and clacking heels and castanets.

OLÉ! I yelled enthusiastically, copying what I had observed in Spain years ago.

Little Truckee had almost never experienced such an exotic performance. My friend Ann had graciously agreed to accompany me, and I had reserved a front row seat. Well, okay, there was only one row. It was a small club, so we were almost close enough to reach out and touch the performers.

So—what does this have to do with back surgery? Just that this is where I was when I realized my back was killing me!

What my doctor told me the following Monday after the X-rays didn't sound good. "Two slipped disks: L-4 and L-5."

"Try physical therapy," she said, "and ibuprofen if the pain gets too bad." Well, anything is better than back surgery, I thought.

With the physical therapists I did the stretching, warm water therapy, manipulation of the spine, special cushions for sitting, lumbar epidural steroid injections for sciatica, and on my own, some meditation. Nothing helped.

I couldn't sit down to dinner in a regular chair like a normal person. To eat dinner I had to lie back on my recliner and with the plate on my chest and try to fork the food in. Peas were especially onerous, rolling off my fork and down to my lap and into the creases of my recliner. *My God, this is worse than my heart attacks and bypass surgery!* But I still held fast to the perception that surgery was still not an option.

I finally resorted to the dreaded pain pills, which turned me into a zombie. So I stopped pain pills except the mild ones—which didn't give me much relief. But at least I kept most of my senses.

However, my only respite—sleeping at night—is hard to do when you're in pain. So I started taking the sleeping aide Ambien. That worked. But I became addicted to it. Could not sleep without it.

The last physical therapist I tried gave me the final word: "There's nothing more I can do for you."

Surgery was the only recourse.

"You don't look seventy-nine," the surgeon said as he showed me the X-rays. "But your spine does." *Ugh!*

So after nearly four months of agony, inactivity and Meals on Wheels, one morning I woke up in the recovery room of Renown Hospital in Reno, Nevada.

My first thought: *I'm alive! . . . I guess the surgery is over, wow! It seems like just a few minutes ago when they were giving me the anesthetic.*

Then I noticed another patient nearby who was accompanied by three policemen. I thought that was amusing. *Hey, I'm recovering with a criminal!*

Then a nurse came and told me, "Mr. Jones, you did great!" That was nice, but what I really wanted to know is if the *surgeon* did great. All I did was lie there like an old piece of lunchmeat.

When they got me to my room, I was glad to see the other bed was empty, because I'd previously had some nightmare hospital roommates.

I told the nurse I was thirsty, but all she gave me at first was a tiny cup of ice to suck on. After I dissolved those, she gave me only a miserly sip of water. *What? Is the drought so bad they're rationing water?* I asked the nurse for more and she hesitated, saying, "Promise you won't overdose?" *Geez, it's water for crud's sake, not crack cocaine!*

Later I disposed handily of a liquid lunch and was thereby qualified to handle a turkey dinner that evening, with all the trimmings!

My doctor had advised me to get up and walk a little as soon after the surgery as I could, so later in the evening, the nurse's aide showed me the only right way for invalids like me to sit up and get out of bed. Then I was rolling, with the IV stand and walker. After a few steps, the aide asked, "Can you make it to the doorway?" I was happy that I could do four laps, there and back; then she made me stop.

If you've ever had surgery, you may remember the sweet aftermath. You just lie there in that wonderful hospital bed and don't have to do a thing. In fact it's impossible, even if you try, because you're hog-tied by intravenous tubes on one or both arms, and you have the pleasure of being connected to a urinal catheter so you don't have to get up to pee. How convenient! Both legs are wrapped in compression pads, deflating and inflating all night long, like a soft lullaby.

You want to get some sleep, so you start repeating your mantra. You finally doze off, then the night nurse comes in. WELL, HELLO THERE, TIME TO CHECK YOUR VITALS!

I managed to get a little shut-eye after that, but was awakened again at 6:00 a.m. by a few noises on the other side of my room. They were interviewing my new roommate. I heard him say he was ". . . 68 years old, five foot four inches, and weighed 180 pounds." He had fallen, broken his hip, and was in extreme pain.

The entire rest of the day that poor guy lay there, alternately moaning and yelping from intermittent jolts of pain. I felt sorry for him. Sometimes he tried to talk to me.

"I wish I hadn't forgotten my hearing aids," he said.

"I can understand that," I answered.

"I said I wish I hadn't forgotten my hearing aids." Meanwhile, since I felt no severe pain, I was getting antsy to get up and walk again. So the nurse unfettered me and walked with me down the hall and back. The walker and IV stand rolled along like constant companions, making a strange looking caravan. It was then I noticed four deputies two doors down from my room—with the criminal I had seen the day before in the recovery room. Rats! The quality of my neighborhood had taken a serious downturn.

I kept bugging my busy nurse to let me get up to pee and to walk until, with some irritation she unshackled me and said I could go by myself, but only with a walker. But this walker was about a Model-T vintage: plain, aluminum, and made a loud, irritating squeal when it rolled, kind of like the old fingernail-on-the-chalk-board shrill. As I passed the deputies, they looked up and frowned. People passing by craned their necks back and covered their tortured eardrums. This contraption had made me a *persona non grata* in the halls of Renown Hospital.

So I went to the nurses' station and asked if they had any WD40.

"Well," they said, "that's not standard equipment," but agreed that I needed something, "before you keep on pushing that squealer." So one of them rummaged around in a drawer and pulled out a tube of . . . something. It looked like some kind of white salve. I applied it to the squeaky wheels, and set off again on my therapeutic stroll.

"That's much better," I heard the nurse say. "That surgery cream really helped!"

Our Medicare dollars put to good use, I thought.

The next day my gracious friend Ellie came from Truckee, and after getting lost in the hospital for a while, took me home. My wonderful son Will had arrived from Sacramento to help me out, and he fixed a delicious fish taco dinner. I was on that road to a smooth recovery.

But that road turned out to be full of pot holes. My Achilles tendons were so sore (from inactivity) that they hurt worse than the surgical site. I had diarrhea, and my ankles were swollen with peripheral edema. The doc said it was caused by a blood clot in my left leg. And then I started having chest pains in the middle of the night, and drove myself to the ER at Tahoe Forest Hospital in Truckee.

After a multitude of tests, they decided that the chest pain was most likely a result of tiny blood flecks from the clot, and they had infiltrated into my lungs, causing the discomfort. The only treatment for this is blood thinner, so they put me on the dreaded rat poison, called *Coumadin*.

(They really do use Coumadin to kill rats. When they eat it, they simply bleed to death.)

After a couple of months I had no more chest pain, got off the rat poison, and started training for the annual Lake Tahoe Half Marathon, which I completed in October. Life was back on track.

However—months later I became afflicted with Atrial Fibrillation, an arrhythmia, and was once more sentenced to a regime of rat poison. But don't despair. I hadn't given up. And that leads to yet another story.

CHAPTER 18
ABLATION: "REMOVAL OF BODY TISSUE"

We six skiers had started the climb on a ski route that I loved so much. Then I felt that dreaded sensation that stops me in my tracks: A general malaise in my core, and a sudden shortness of breath. Every step uphill was misery, I just wanted to quit and lie down in the snow.

For me, today's excursion was a bust. I was finished, worthless. "I've got to go back," I yelled to the little group ahead.

"What's the matter?"

"My heart just jumped into A-fib. I feel awful. I can't go any farther."

My faithful ski buddy John came over and gave me a hug. "Sorry, man, you gonna be okay?"

"Yeah, I just have to take it easy and get myself home."

It was unfortunate, not only for me, but also for them that I was the one to drop out that day, because I was the only one of the group who knew the exact route. The next day John told me that they took a wrong turn and had to backtrack. It was starting to get dark shortly before they got to their cars.

This attack of A-fib (atrial fibrillation) wasn't the first. Formerly these episodes occurred so seldom that they didn't interfere much with my daily activities. Then they became more frequent, coming suddenly and unpredictably.

A-fib is a form of arrhythmia, an irregular heartbeat. When this affliction was at its most severe, it felt like a wild squirrel was scrambling around in my chest cavity.

When I related these events to the nurse in the cardiac rehab program I had been attending, she informed me that they have a procedure called *ablation* that is supposed to deal with atrial fibrillation. "Does it stop it?" I asked.

"Yes," she said, ". . . well usually."

Usually? That didn't sound terribly reassuring. I looked up the word *ablation*. One definition read: "To gradually remove material from or erode by melting, evaporation, frictional action."

That can't be right. But then I found another description: "The removal of body tissue." What body tissue do they remove? How do they remove it? Finally one source did also say that it was used "to treat atrial fibrillation. But I still had questions. Did I really want to donate some body tissue? One day on a hike with my son Brian and his kids, I had to stop and pull the same old *I have to go back* routine. Brian, more accustomed to my *let's go* mode, looked at me. "You're going to have to do something about this," he said. "It's impacting your lifestyle."

He was right. And not only that. My doctors had put me back on the dreaded blood thinner, Coumadin, the only treatment for this condition. Although A-fib isn't life threatening, anyone afflicted with it is more subject to strokes. The only kind of stroke I ever want is one of good fortune or genius. So I started taking the rat poison again. Once more I would have to get a supply of band aids; all sizes, for every little cut or scrape.

It was time to start looking for a doctor who specialized in performing the ablation procedure.

"Yes," Dr. Stark said, after considerable interrogation and examination, "you are a viable candidate for this procedure."

I soon learned that to accomplish this procedure, the doctor has to run two wires up from the groin, on both sides, to the heart. Then they burn or freeze the areas in the heart that have been causing the electric malfunctions. Those affected parts are history. Scars. Dead meat. So this is what "removal of tissue" means. They kill it.

I vacillated a bit. *Is it worth it? Yeah, I'll do it. At least they don't have to cut me open like they did with my bypass.* What I didn't know was that the procedure would take *four hours* under general anesthesia. That's twice as long as my open heart surgery took.

I felt pretty crappy when it was done, but Dr. Stark said encouragingly, "Usually it's only a one night stay." I wanted to get out of there, so even though I felt like the proverbial "pulled backwards through a knot hole," I went home the next afternoon.

That night I felt horrible. Chest pain and other indescribables. At around 2:00 a.m., in a panic, I called my son Will. "What do you want to do?" he asked. I didn't know, but then I saw a phone number on the discharge papers that was Dr. Starks emergency number. Thankfully he answered Will's call.

Back in the hospital, I had a few complications, such as low blood pressure, and abnormal kidney readings. But those didn't last, and I went home the next day— with normal heart rhythm!

But . . . it only lasted two days, then went back into arrhythmia. Dr. Stark then recommended a *cardio version*. That's an electric shock. It kicked my heart back into normal rhythm—for a couple of weeks, then it came back as "*A-flutter,*" less intense than "A-fib," but still arrhythmia. It continued intermittently.

"You need another ablation," my doctor the tormentor told me, "so we can fix what we missed." I thought of a bunch of dirty words, but said, "Okay, I guess we'd better finish the job."

The night before I was to check into the hospital again for another ablation, I started vomiting at 3:30 a.m. The *Norovirus* had swooped into our facility like a Viking raid.

Weeks later, I endured the second ablation, also lasting four hours. It went off okay except that afterward the male nurse turned me over carelessly after insisting that I lie still on my back without moving to prevent bleeding. But his actions started all over again.

"Oh. . ." he said, "lie still two more hours, then . . . be careful!"

I would see that he was flogged when I got out. But when that happened, I was too happy with my newly gained sinus rhythm (normal) to worry about retribution.

Yet once again, it only lasted for a while. "We'll do another *cardio version*," my doc said cheerily, "that should work this time." *Promises, promises.*

But it did work! That was on April 16, 2011, and since then I have been working out at the gym, hiking, climbing at altitudes over 8,000-foot elevations, as well as dancing the polka and Lindy hop.

Then, after a year free of A-fib, my cardiologist took me off of the nasty blood thinner. I felt free as a bird!

After this second ablation I only had one minor complication: the insertion points were leaking a little fluid. Nothing serious, but I saw that the moisture had seeped into the crotch of my trousers and . . . well, you know what that looked like. So before going down to the dining room for lunch, I stuffed an old T-shirt in my pants to soak up any secretion. That got me a bit more attention than I wanted, but I had the impression that some of the ladies looked at me more appreciatively than before.

Well . . . you might ask . . . the ablation . . . was it worth it to put up with these procedures, complications, cardioversions, and other crap?

Damn straight it was!!

Chapter 19
Adventures With
the Old Folks

When I moved from my life of mountaineering in the Sierra to live with the old folks (they were old, but I wasn't—ha!), it was an adjustment, and I was compelled to write about the contrast between my old life with young, athletic people and my new life with a whole different pace.

My first book about this topic is titled *Surviving the Old Folks' Home,* and the second is *Memoirs of the Old Folks' Home in the Time of COVID and Trump.* (A historical document, don't miss it.)

But just because those books are already published, doesn't mean that stuff here in this place stopped happening. So I'm once again writing about the crazy capers that are taking place currently. So, these stories are fresh and I serve them hot off the geriatric griddle!

If you don't believe there is material here, listen to the words of our new business manager:

"When I first came here to work," she said, "I thought, 'Just some old souls sitting in the atrium doing nothing—some not even talking. An old guy walks by, stooped over a walker; another in a wheelchair. Nothing much going on here, I bet.' But boy, was I wrong!"

Behind this passive scene, sparks of ardor, frustration, joy, pain, contentment, and hilarity may flare up at any time. It is a geriatric microcosm of our society with some memory loss thrown in. Do you really want to know what's going on in such a domicile? Be careful what you ask for!

[The characters described are real people, but I have not used their real names.]

MOLLIE AND TOMMY

"Yeah," Deirdre explains, "while Mollie's husband was dying of cancer in their apartment downstairs, Mollie was screwing around with Tommy in his apartment on the second floor."

Tommy had been looking for a "cuddle bunny" since he first moved in. When he approached ladies with that hope, the answer he usually got was, "Well, don't look at me!" But then he met sweet little Mollie.

She is a jolly little lady, about five feet tall and what some, especially Tommy, would call "pleasingly plump." She dresses well, often in newly pressed pants suits and a smile.

When Tommy swooped in on Mollie, the fact that she had a husband didn't seem to enter into the equation. I guess their thinking was—well, I don't know what they were thinking. Maybe just the modern concept of *friends with benefits? Life is too short to resist hanky-panky when it's available?*

But then the spikes of the ugly corona virus required a lockdown, which interrupted their capers, and Tommy's family moved him out to keep him safe. Not only from the virus, but also from that perceived grasping woman. Tommy was deprived, Mollie was devastated. Then Mollie's husband died.

But Mollie revitalized herself and became a cheerleader at some of our competitive games such as Ladder Golf and Bean Bag Baseball. Her applause and words of encouragement were much appreciated. But one night she took a fall and had to go into Assisted Living. We had liked her—and now we miss her. And Tommy is just ancient history.

SUNDOWN AT CREEKSIDE

Daytime, Abigail appears to be normal, a nice lady. But as the light fades, her world dims, and she descends into confusion and distrust. Darkness and shadows can distort a mind. Abigail metamorphoses into a bewildered paranoiac. She wanders aimlessly, consumed with fear and suspicion.

I can't even imagine how awful it must be to be plunged into such disorientation with each nightfall.

Dora, who occupies the apartment right under Abigail, complains that she is often awakened by the scraping of furniture that Abigail moves each night to block her doorway against perceived transgressors. When staff members come to Abigail's room to aid or check on her, it's difficult to enter her room with a heavy chest of drawers holding the door shut.

One evening, neighbor Dora saw Abigail pick up a chair and throw it against the window pane on the second floor, trying to create an exit. "I've got to get out of here!" she exclaimed. Fortunately the window glass didn't break, and Dora was able to calm Abigail down. She took her downstairs to the concierge, who pointed out the front exit, but assured her that she didn't have to leave because they would protect her.

Another night Abigail reported to the concierge that "a man is in my apartment and I want you to get him out of there." So the concierge dutifully went up to her apartment and shooed away the imaginary man to satisfy Abigail.

Finally we were happy to see that Abigail moved to a memory care facility where she can get the help and attention she needs.

ALZHEIMER'S IN INDEPENDENT LIVING

Her name is Skylar and she's relatively harmless. Or so we thought until she contracted COVID and couldn't remember to stay isolated in her room. She is actually a sweet, attractive lady but she's good at getting herself in some unfortunate predicaments when her Alzheimer's runs amuck. She wanders in the hallway, and asks, "Will you show me where my room is?"

But worse is when she's wandering loose in various states of undress. Her next-door neighbor described it this way: "There she was, starting to go downstairs, wearing only a short T-shirt—that's all! She was holding a wet Depends in one hand. 'Oh, honey,' I told her, 'You need to go back to your apartment and put some clothes on!'"

"Well, what do I do with this?" Skylar said defensively, holding out her hand as the muck from the used *Depends* dribbled through her fingers to the floor.

Residents learn to lock their doors when they leave their apartments. One evening when Aurora returned to her room, there was Skylar, in her nightgown on Aurora's bed. "What are you doing here on my bed?" Aurora gasps.

"Well, I thought this was my bed," answered Skylar.

"No," said Aurora, "This is definitely my bed."

"Well, there's room for both of us," said Skylar. She has a sense of humor. Aurora then had to call the concierge to come and take Skylar to her own room. Although we get our chuckles, it's not that funny. It's sad, and should not take place in an Independent Living Facility. These poor souls should be in Memory Care or someplace where they get the attention they need. But the problem is often because some family members don't want or are unable to pay the big bucks that the extra care requires. Evidently our corporation does not have the legal authority to expel them. So we look after them as best we can.

HOW CHEAP IS HE?

It takes all kinds right? We have the generous, the giving, the unselfish. Then there are others who are *tight as a duck's arse.* Our resident skinflint is tall and skinny, so we call him Slim.

Slim is cordial, approachable, and easy to talk to—except when he gets going on about the stock market and how much he is earning or losing. He hints that he is worth a small fortune.

But he is the *cheapest* person we've ever seen. *How cheap is he?* He is *so* cheap that one day he ordered a take-out meal from our dining room just before going out for lunch with a friend. I wish I could have seen the waiter's expression when Slim pulled out his bring-along lunch and started munching.

When we have free swap meets here, frugal-to-a-fault Slim gets there early to pick out the best items—to sell on eBay. No matter what it is, anything that's labeled *FREE* sucks him in like a horny buck deer to a doe in season.

Slim went to a bank to change his coins to bills even though he has no account there. A witness

"WHAT?"

Dan repeated, and Ben dug in his pocket and brought out paper and pen.

"Okay," Dan said, "What time is my appointment?"

"Two p.m.," I said, "but you have to take the bus at 1:30."

Suddenly the PA system rattled to life. The manager announced that the elevator would be out of service the next day between nine and eleven a.m.

"WHAT DID HE SAY?" Ben asked me, and I repeated the information.

Then Dan asked, "Is my doctor appointment today or tomorrow?"

"Tomorrow . . . at two p.m. You wrote it down."

"Oh, good, yeah, okay, I've got it here someplace." He finds the little piece of paper in a pocket.

"So keep ahold of that, okay? See you later," and I started walking away. But I could still hear Ben asking Dan, "WHEN DID HE SAY THE ELEVATOR WOULDN'T BE WORKING?"

"I don't remember," Dan replied.

Ben turned to the next table and yelled, "WHAT ARE THE HOURS WE CAN'T USE THE ELEVATOR?"

"Between nine and eleven," a guy answered very loudly.

Dan turned to Ben. "Is that today or tomorrow?"

"WHAT?" Ben said, and Dan raised his voice and repeated the question.

Ben asked the next table again, "IS THAT TODAY OR TOMORROW?'

And so it goes. These guys aren't stupid. They just have a little impairment. Like me, when I walked up to Mary in my Mr. Magoo mode, and said, "Good morning, Sally."

DAN AND SKYLAR

Dan is a likable guy. And with his poor memory retention, he and Alzheimer-lady Skylar make a good match.

One afternoon I was checking my mail and saw Dan and Skylar sitting together on the couch in the atrium, so I walked over to say hello.

Dan addressed me, "Have you met Skylar? She's kinda my . . . neighbor."

Well, I had met Skylar, of course, had seen her a hundred times, and even exchanged brief bits of conversation. But I shook her hand and said "hi" anyway. I thought it was strange she offered her left hand. Then I saw that her right hand was busy—holding Dan's hand. Hmm, this is new. These two an item now? Does that poor lady know what she's doing? Does Dan?

As I said before, I think Dan is a good guy. But according to some of the ladies, they view him in a different light . . . and it's not a very rosy one.

"He came up to me," Dora said, "and told me what nice breasts I have . . . and that he admired my nice figure! It's inappropriate to say stuff like that."

"Oh, yeah," added Stella, "I learned from the first to keep away from him."

"Right," Sophia chimed in, "I just don't trust him."
"You know," Stella added, "I've read that some guys who have dementia have a tendency to be really . . . horny."

"I believe it," said Dora, "At the New Year's Eve party, Dan and Skylar left the dance and sneaked into the empty dining room. He had his hands all over her!" Yup, folks just another day at Creekside High. Gossip. Rumors. You don't know what to believe. Dan is no longer here. Sex drive or not, he was a good guy and we guys miss him.

THE FOLLIES OF HALLOWEEN

We were getting ready. Our Activities Director, Amanda, had erected a fake spider web overhead in the atrium. She had a bunch of plastic black spiders that we were throwing up into the web to create more of a spooky ambience. Sometimes the spiders didn't stick, so we picked them up and gave them another toss. It was kind of silly, but fun. Several residents walked by to watch and take in the holiday atmosphere.

Then *Queen Aubrey* made her regal entrance and was observing what her subjects were doing. Not that she was willing to lower herself to participate in such a proletarian pursuit.

Aubrey earned the moniker *Queen* surreptitiously because of all her incredible accomplishments, the majority of which she freely loaded upon us: She formerly worked for the FBI and CIA in "very important positions" that she couldn't tell us about. "I know so much you would be amazed, but I'm sworn to secrecy."

She is "very rich" and "loves to drive" her new Mercedes. Her marvelous children are all "brilliant and own prime real estate that is worth, oh, more than I can say." And she herself owns eight or nine enterprises, which she does not name.

Aubrey therefore feels that she should have special privileges here at Creekside Oaks. At lunch, she holds court at a table with a nice location near the window, which gives her a great view of the royal parking lot. You have to pass muster to be able to join her at her table, but I don't know what the necessary prerequisites are.

She originally insisted that "her" table should be reserved for her alone, but the manager told her right out that "there are no reserved tables here." So she just comes early and plunks herself down.

So, back to Halloween and the spider web. Aubrey, on the way back from her hair dresser with a perfect new *do*, was standing there watching the bustle with mild interest before retiring to her penthouse apartment up on the third floor. Sophia was standing right behind her with a spider in her hand. Then instead of getting the spider into the web, she impulsively dropped it into Aubrey's impeccable coiffeur. And there it stuck, unbeknownst to the Queen.

Gradually ripples of muffled laughter spread around the room as people saw or heard what had happened.

Sometime later Amanda approached Aubrey from behind and said, "Aubrey, you have a spider in your hair," and picked it out and showed it to her.

"OH, NO!" Aubrey was horrified.

"Don't worry, it's just a fake spider. Must have fallen from the web."

Afterwards, Amanda told us, "She (the queen) was very upset."

But it just sweetened our Halloween that much more. And I usually don't even like Halloween.

PARTY TABLE

Doris smiles as she walks by our table at lunchtime. "So," she says, "I think this is the fun table, here, Huh?"

"Yes," I say, "but I think maybe some of these people get irritated by all our joyful ruckus."

"Oh, phooey on them," Doris says, "If you're laughing it means you're just having a good time. Nothing wrong with that!"

And she's right. We're the noisiest and happiest bunch in our dining room as far as I can tell. Many of our conversations lead to hilarity and occasionally turning to some degree of buffoonery. That's why we call ourselves — *The Party Table!*

Here's an example of our daily discourse:

Barry: "I admire the good posture of that new lady on the second floor. When she walks she keeps her head up and is so erect.

Luna: "Well, she just about has to hold herself up straight so that those big boobs of hers don't weigh her down and pull her over."

Rodrigo: "Yes, she's stacked. Did you notice?"

Barry: "Yeah, sure, I noticed."

Rodrigo: "I was talking to Sophia."

Sophia: "Yes, I know, but I don't pay so much attention to those things like you guys do. And you know, this can be a major problem for some women. If their breasts get too big, it can complicate daily activities with those ponderous things swinging around with every step."

Rodrigo: "Well . . . okay, so now, I finally know what *sports bras* are for anyway."

Barry: "Yes, I've herd about women having surgery for breast reduction."

Sophia, smiling as she looks around: "I wonder if anyone is overhearing our boob conversation."

Barry: "Probably, but so far I've heard nothing but a little tittering . . . that's most likely because we were having such a titillating conversation."

Sophia (giggling): "Enough guys, okay? I'm trying to eat my lunch here."

—◇—

And some days ninety-seven-year-old Luna regales us with her irreverent and sometimes risqué tales about her job as a nurse's aide in a hospital.

"I loved my job," she exclaims, adding that she was often assigned to the men's psychiatric ward. The episodes flow out of her mouth with gleeful ease: "A man came in who had been diagnosed with a traumatic penis amputation at age six." (Rodrigo and I winced at the thought.) Evidently this poor guy had kept a positive attitude, because after the first night there, he told Luna: "Last night I dreamed about you. I was Errol Flynn and you were Olivia de Havilland, and we made love sixty-six times."

Luna said she answered, "No wonder I'm so tired this morning!"

Then she told us about this poor demented guy, who stuffed a pencil up his penis. (Ouch!) She related that the doctors were discussing the pencil-penis case later, and a lady who had just given birth to a baby girl, overheard him as he described to his colleague this strange action: "Yes, right into his urethra! I couldn't believe it!"

All the mother with the baby girl heard was "urethra," and thought they were referring to a woman standing nearby.

"Oh, what a beautiful name! I think I'll name my daughter! Urethra!"

—◇—

Since Rodrigo and I are both fascinated with language, we often discuss vocabulary. I was saying that once, when I used the word crotch, referring to the fork of a tree, my kids scoffed and thought I was being a smart ass, because they hadn't heard the word used in that context. To them, crotch, was that part of the body there between our legs.

"No, no," I corrected them, "crotch is the proper term to use when referring to the area of the tree where the trunk branches up into two parts."

"So," I asked the others, "is crotch the origin of the word crotchety—meaning irritable?"

"That doesn't make sense," Rodrigo said, "What does crotch have to do with being irritable?"

"Well, language works in mysterious ways," I said.

"Hey," Sophia ventured, "I wonder how many crotches an octopus has?"

"Well, eight, I guess," said Dora.

"No," Rodrigo said, "wouldn't it be just seven actual crotches?"

Then we stopped and looked at each other. "This may be the dumbest conversation we've ever had here," Sophia then suggested. We all nodded and searched for another topic.

Both Dora and I were dealing with migrational swallows that had set up residence on our outside balconies.

"God, they make a mess," Dora complained, "I can't hardly even sit out on my patio."

"Yeah," I said, "and my swallows built their nest right above my screen door, so to go out onto my balcony, I have to make a really wide step to avoid their droppings."

"And they crap all over my windows!" Dora added.

Yes, it is an inconvenience, and at times even a little disgusting, but we agreed that it is important to protect nature's species, especially the endangered ones. Swallows are included in that category, so it would be illegal to knock down the nests.

Then Rodrigo reminded us that he lived on the first floor, and that's why he finds quite a few critters that come into his apartment without invitation.

"But in line with our respect for nature's inhabitants," Rodrigo said, "yesterday I found a cockroach in my living room. So I got it into a little jar, then gave it a crumb to eat and took it outside and let it out on the other side of the bike path."

"Ha," Sophia joked, "How do you know he didn't tell his friends that he found a place that gives him food, so then they come back in full force?"

"No, they won't," Rodrigo protested. "And, hey I also found a little lizard on the floor behind the couch. I told it gently that I wouldn't harm it, I just wanted him to leave. I pulled the couch out a little to make room for him to exit. Pretty soon it scrambled out from behind the couch so I propped the outside door open and it went out."

We didn't know what to say about that. Live and let live, I suppose.

—◇—

"Why don't you like Helen?" I asked Rodrigo one day. Helen is a sweet little Korean lady who walks slowly around the dining room, wondering if it is breakfast or lunch.

"Well," Rodrigo responds, "every time I sit with my friends Veronica and James, she scolds me. For some reason she thinks I'm married: So she keeps admonishing me, "Why don't you sit with your own wife?!"

Confusion reigns in paradise.

During football season, Luna gets a little frustrated, because she doesn't understand the game.

"All I know," Luna says, "is that if the ball goes through those posts, it gets some points. And if they get the ball over the line at the end of the field, it's a touchdown. Then they all get in a huddle and pat each others bottoms."

—◇—

Then there's Ezekiel. He is very religious and sometimes preaches and tries to convert unaware fellow residents. The he tells the female servers, "You should have long hair, and let it hang down, not keep it all tied up in a knot." The manager points out that it is to keep their hair from getting in your food. "Well," Ezekiel maintains, "God wants boys to have short hair, and girls long hair."

Ezekiel has is own ideas about dress and grooming for the kitchen employees. He insists that our chef and servers should wear white shirts. "Here's some money," he tells server Jason, "Go buy a white shirt."

Even worse, Ezekiel is a *creamaholic.* He can't get enough French vanilla coffee creamer. One morning he goes around to five tables, and steals the little pitcher of French vanilla creamer that is for that table.

"You're a thief!" Luna yells to him.

But Ezekiel, unrepentant, said, "I have to have my French vanilla! Then he orders a full cup of it from a server, smiles and raises it up to his quivering lips. Luna says she is tempted to ask him, "What would Jesus say?"

And Ezekiel has other issues as well. He suggested that the female servers should all wear Barbie Doll costumes.

Whenever we have a new male server, he thinks they are "unionizers" and tells the chef he should fire him.

Like I said, it takes all kinds. And we have 'em.

Chapter 20
Elders Beating the Odds Playing Baseball

"What do you mean, you couldn't leave?" I chided our company bus driver. "I said I'd be ready to be picked up at 3:15."

"Sorry, I just got caught up in the drama of the baseball game back at the home," she said, "The score was tied and then Team One got a homer!"

Yes, I could well imagine that scene there in the senior community where I live. *Team One is six runs ahead. But Team Two is up to bat and it's the last inning. Shouts of encouragement abound and the air is electric with anticipation. Can they tie up the game?*

But as I relate this, I suspect there is some skepticism on the part of you, the reader. How can a bunch of old farts play an energetic game like baseball? This over-the-hill gang—some half blind, others hobbling with canes, shuffling along with walkers, or even confined to a wheelchair. Some of the rest shamble along like old horses coming in to the barn after a hard day of plowing. How can these old folks bat balls and run bases?

Well, kids, we can do it because it's *beanbag baseball,* and we more than meet the challenge. Here's how it works: We divide into two teams, which makes for a competitive feel that whips up emotions and charges the atmosphere. We throw beanbags at a big board with holes in it.

The first time I saw that big white board filled with holes we were supposed to hit with the bean bags, I said, *no way can I play this game. I can't see where the hell I should throw the damn things!* But then I walked up and stuck my head right in its holey face. That way I was able to read the labels, and I got a sense of where to aim if I wanted to hit the home run hole or a base. But it was tricky. The two out holes flanked the homer hole. The holes for the three bases were scattered around the board.

When the game is going strong, and the number of runs each team has is close, the noise level picks up as the competitive juices start heating up. Everyone wants to do well and help their team. Pressure mounts. The chairs that serve as bases are loaded, and the runners are anxious for their teammate to bring them home.

The unthinkable is for the bean bag thrower to get an *OUT,* especially if it would be the third OUT. "Come on, you can do it!" we might yell to spirit up the person at bat.

Suspense . . . then . . . Home run! Pandemonium! You'd be surprised how much rowdy racket these elder guys and gals can make when they're excited.

Or, maybe they got an—OUT! Muffled groans of disappointment. Heads down with resignation. But only momentarily, because these folks are having a good time. It's just a game, not brain surgery.

Becca, our entertainment director, sets the game up and manages it. She encourages all comers, regardless of any mental or physical handicap.

Like Noah, who is just one of the crowd with a hitch in his get-along. We admire him as he awkwardly maneuvers his walker into position to throw his first bean bag. Whoops! It goes wild, sailing over the top of the board. "That's okay," Becca insists. And Noah gradually gets the feel of it, starts hitting bases and home runs. And then he limps along determinedly behind his ancient walker to every base into home for a score. You can tell he feels good about it.

The best players are the oldest guys. Cruz, for example, is ninety-six, and a combat veteran of World War II. He is always attired in nicely pressed pants and shirt and a smile. He probably gets more homers in this game than anyone. If he makes a bad toss, he scolds himself gently: "A little higher, Cruzerino!" On the rare occasion that he doesn't play up to par, he accepts it in good humor, saying in a soft voice, "Just not my day, I guess."

Then there's Oscar, another consistently good player. He is ninety-four and looks it, with a leathery, wrinkled face, hearing aids, and glasses—and his portable oxygen tank. When he steps up to toss the bags, he is intent and often hits a home run. But if he does, he is allowed not to run the bases, because with any little exertion he gets out of breath.

If Oscar makes a bad play, we see him set his mouth in disgust, and shake his head, as though saying, *what is wrong with me!*

Oscar has had a full life, and is still living it. Besides baseball, he plays ladder golf, bocce ball, poker, pool and the piano. And he is tough. He has to be. He is the oldest known heart transplant patient in the nation. His favorite song is "I Left My Heart in San Francisco," where he had the surgery so many years ago.

My friend Camila, one of our younger residents—seventies, low eighties? Who knows?—she may not remember what she had for breakfast, but she is fun, capable, and down to earth. She always seems happy and has a delightful laugh. She has preserved much of her good looks from earlier days, and she's a talented player.

When Camila is up to bat, Oscar likes to heckle her a little: "Hubba hubba," he says, as Camila is about to make a toss.

"Oh, really?" Camila turns around and glares at him in mock disgust. "That's enough from the peanut gallery." As she winds up to pitch, Oscar mumbles another "hubba," and Camila stops in mid swing. "Hey, we have women's lib now, you know. You better catch up!" Then she scores a home run, turns to face Oscar, chin up, and swaying with a little victory dance. The corners of Oscar's mouth angle up; he chuckles and applauds Camila with the rest of us. We relish all this *faux drama.*

Regina is a feisty little ninety-eight-year-old. Her arthritic back keeps her upper body bent forward, and her eyes seem to be in a constant squint. In spite of all that, she is in remarkably good shape.

When she gets a permanent on her tightly curled white hair, she admits she looks like a Q-Tip. We don't argue, and she's undaunted.

Although Regina is known to use colorful language at times, she usually doesn't swear. When she gets disgusted with a bad throw, she says, "DIRTY WORD!" as a substitute expletive.

Regina is legally blind and often when it's her turn to try her luck with the bean bags, she says, "It sure would be nice to see what I'm throwing at!" I know how she feels.

And do you remember Dan? Nice fella with dementia, and sweet Skylar, who has Alzheimer's Disease? Well, the latest rumor is that they have been sharing beds. But who cares?

Anyway, one day they came to play baseball. "You stand right here, honey," Becca explains to Skylar, "and try to throw the bag in the middle." After hitting the floor and then a foul, Skylar gets a second base, so Becca leads her to the right chair amid rousing applause.

Dan, after a wild pitch, gets third base, then just sits down, so Becca has to lead him around the bases.

These two keep Becca pretty busy, but it's good to see them involved. we see it as an added attraction.

Leah and Larry often come to the baseball game. They both have walkers and sit together. Leah has a bald spot in the top back of her head. It doesn't matter though, as she can't see it, and we just pretend that we don't either. Leah is a nice lady, friendly and cheerful.

Larry usually plays the game, but Leah is always just a spectator, and that's fine.

When she transfers from her walker to a cushy chair, she is there for the duration, happy as a kitten in a cozy corner.

One day Becca invited Leah to get up and participate in the game. *Fat chance,* we thought. "Oh, no," Leah shakes her head, "I don't think so."

But Becca strives to get as many people as possible involved in our fun stuff, so she persists. "Oh, I bet you can do it, c'mon, Leah, let's try." Becca helps her stand, and after three tries, she makes it, and grabs her walker, and Becca leads her over to home plate.

Leah's first toss goes sailing clear over to no-man's-land. "That's okay," Becca said, "just look at the bases on the board and throw at them." Leah hits third base! "Wonderful!" exclaims Becca. "But you don't have to run the bases, we'll excuse you from that. But Leah is really into it now, and insists on going to each base, nudging each chair base with her walker, grinning like a home run queen. And later, she did hit a homer, and we rewarded her with lusty cheers.

We have no shortage here of folks who divert us with their unique personas. Ava, for example, is a tiny lady with great determination. She has a disease which affects her voice and mobility. But don't underestimate her. She writes poetry and occasionally reads some verses in honor of a resident who has passed. And she doesn't shy away from tossing a few beanbags.

When she comes up to home plate to make her toss, she takes a while to get positioned. Grasping her walker, she rotates around, taking a series of rapid, tiny staccato steps, making an arc order to face the board. It's a bit mesmerizing to watch this process, and we laud her resolve.

Becca hands her a beanbag, but Ava looks at Camila and her lips move, but her voice is so faint, Camila, who can't hear her, shakes her head, so Eva turns back and tosses the beanbag.

Another game we play is Ladder Golf. We throw three tennis balls connected by a string at a little ladder for points. Talk of balls engender numerous salacious remarks and much hilarity. For example: "Does everyone have balls?" Dan doesn't have any balls.

"Richard, you share with Don and use his balls." Becca has had to learn to phrase her *balls* questions very carefully.

Then Oscar, always a cutup, stands, holds his oxygen in one hand, and dangles his tennis balls in front of him below his belt. The crowd cracks up.

But due to the competitive nature of opposing teams, our beanbag baseball generates the most noise and enthusiasm. Besides, some of these old folks have gotten pretty good. I have read that some senior communities have entered the annual Senior Summer Beanbag Games. I watched a video of seniors performing in Reno. They wore uniforms and were good at hitting the mark. But I didn't see any walkers, canes or power chairs. They were old, but able bodied and they could see what they were throwing at. So maybe we could sponsor our own event, kind of like the ParaOlympics. We could call it the Croakside Oaks Para-old-folks Summer Games. What do you think?

CHAPTER 21
FUN WITH FITNESS FOLKS

When you first enter the building, the sounds you pick up may be the sporadic guffaws of camaraderie from some of the young hard bodies. They're telling each other bad jokes, or relating their most recent failed romantic exploits.

Or you may hear the wheezing and gurgling of the hydra-massage chair, as the water within rumbles and tickles the spine of the occupant who is stretched out, eyes closed with an air of relief and contentment.

This is California Family Fitness, a huge, two-story building, with so many exercise devices that you wonder what kind of deranged minds would contrive such an abundance of instruments that can put to the test every muscle, nerve and joint in your mortal body.

Herein you can find a tendon extension machine, a Romanian Dead Lift, and everything in between. We can enjoy three swimming pools including a lap pool, hot tub, and sauna.

This edifice is big enough to house basketball and racquetball courts, as well as a complete physical therapy unit.

As a bonus, besides getting a workout, it's a great place for people watching. In the weight lifting section, you can see some hefty guys handling ridiculously massive loads, often accompanied by violent bellows, which I suppose is an essential part of lifting that monstrous barbell up above one's head. Then they drop it, making a heck of a racket, and causing reverberations in the flooring. Tough guys, tough floors, but abused eardrums.

But it's not just macho guys who hang out in this complex. Over a third of these fitness buffs are female. The presence of these young ladies, dressed in neat apparel such as tights or shorts enhance the general atmosphere of the place. Their pleasant fragrances counter nicely the heavy scent of machismo. I look around with regret that I didn't frequent venues such as this in my youth. But as I reflect more deeply, I realize that when I was young, there were very few such establishments and if there were, it would not be considered proper or normal for young ladies to frequent such places.

Here, it's a treat to see petite gals pumping iron along with their young male counterparts. Good for them! I say.

Most of my fellow residents here in *the home* don't understand why anyone living in an old folks' home would go and "pump iron." The usual reaction is "Well, don't overdo it!" They are unaware that besides the weights, we practice balance, stretch all our joints and muscles, swim in summertime, and take advantage of the cardio machines that are designed to be easy on the joints, as opposed to running.

I tried to describe to a lady here a movement I do to help my balance: "I stand on one foot," I said, "while swinging the other foot back and forth in front of the stationary foot."

"But isn't that embarrassing?" she asks. "Don't people stare at you?"

"Heck no. They're busy doing their own thing, possibly something a lot more bizarre than what I do. And if anyone is ever watching, it's surreptitiously."

However, once in a while, some of my fellow members admittedly do provide some unexpected entertainment. One guy jogs on his tippy toes. He looks like an oversized toddler running away from mommy.

Another character walks down the aisle exercising his arms by waving them up and down like wings. I resist the temptation to ask him, "Having trouble getting airborne?"

Then my attention is drawn to a head popping up in the air on the other side of the aerobic machines. Then it's gone . . . then it bobs up again. What the heck? So I go around and see this guy shooting baskets. It looks like he's practicing repeated jump shots. But without a ball. That's right! He had no balls.

As you walk around you may notice some young woman on her back in the stretching area executing the upward pelvic motion. It's a common stretch, yet worthy of a second glance.

You can catch a little drama if you happen to watch the super athlete I call "Mr. Fitness." He knows he's good. Gee, I wonder what it's like to be so positively proud of oneself? He saunters over to the stretching area, preening, with a wide smile on his face, like an actor going on stage for his number. He performs his specialty, the split squat jump. That is a hard move and he does it marvelously.

Some people work with *the snake,* which is a long, black tube about three inches in diameter, secured at one end.

You're supposed to take the loose end and shake it violently, like you would a garden hose that you were trying to shake loose from a bush.

But even noisier and weirder is seeing a guy pick up a ball the size of a basketball, but it's solid and heavy. He brings it up over his head, then slams it down on the floor with all his strength. It reminds me of someone having a temper tantrum.

But evidently that didn't assuage his frustrations, because then he picks it up and slams it violently against the wall. It makes such a big bang that it resounds across the room. You wonder if he's working off his stresses. But it's just fitness.

Then there's the *vocal* guy, who has to yell with each move: "OH, AH, HUH, MY GOD." Then he races over and does some quick stepping, and pushups, letting us know how hard he's workings he bellows "EEYA, WOW, JEEZ, SHIT . . . oh, sorry."

But now let's give credit to the gal who's working out on the Romanian Dead Lift, a device that's more commonly used by some brawny man. This lady is attractive, not big, but not small. As she lifts up that dead weight, you can detect her great muscle definition. Her face shows defiance and determination as she strains to get the weight up higher. She is very strong and very feminine.

It's also impressive to witness other feats of amazing athleticism. Like the young men and women who, from a standing position on the floor, jump up in one leap to land on a surface in front of them four or more feet higher. This is another giant leap for mankind. Wow! And womankind too.

But the winner is the rope jumper. The rope moves so fast it is invisible, as are his feet. He does every combination possible, cross armed sometimes, one foot, two feet, alternating, changing cadences. He looks professional to me, and he's right here in our little ol' Folsom gym.

Then there are times when I, myself, seem to be the object of . . . not admiration, but rather curiosity. One day I was merely executing a recommended stretch for my Achilles tendon, and it had to be done on a stair step, easing the heel down lower than the rest of the foot.

So I was on the bottom step of the second floor staircase, looking upward, but pressing that heel down. I guess it looked like I was just longing to be able to walk upstairs, because, at different times three people offered to help me up to the second floor.

To avoid this unwanted attention, the following day I went up to the next to the top step to stretch. This time I got, "Oh, you can do it, you're almost there, just one more step!"

The other times I might be noticed is when I'm walking from the StairMaster to the elliptical cardio machine wearing my headphones, listening to a polka and moving to the beat. And at times I forget that I'm not in my little private space just because I have my headphones on, so I may sing along.

I haven't met a lot of people here, but know a few that I also see at Arthur Murray dance center. Then there's this friendly guy, maybe 40s, great muscular physique, who greets me like he knows me, so I reciprocate, even though I have no idea who he is or why he addresses me.

And there's Denise, a pretty sixty-year-old, who came up one day to tell me how she admired me for coming here and working out at my age. I don't know how she found out I was old.

And then . . . there was . . . Esther. But that's a whole other story.

CHAPTER 22
ESTHER

"Hi there, it's so good to see you today." She was perky, petite, pretty—and young. In her thirties maybe, forties max.

"Well, hello," I said, wondering who she was, and why she acted like she knew me. Is she one of the young servers in our senior dining room? Or someone I'd danced with at the Arthur Murray studio?

"I haven't seen you for a few days," she continued.

"Yeah, I missed a couple of workouts," I said. "So—where do I know you from?"

"Here," she said emphatically. "I see you all the time and you are an inspiration. Me, I have to push myself to come, but every time, here you are, going strong . . . uh, my name is Esther."

"Oh, Esther is my mother's name!"

"Well, I'm not surprised," she said.

What did she mean by that? I introduced myself, and we proceeded to chat. She was easy to talk to, and in no hurry to move on. We shared information about each other that was unusual for two people who have just met.

"I have cancer," she admitted. "I went to Israel and it got better, but now it seems to be coming back."

"Oh, I'm so sorry . . . me, I'm into dancing at Arthur Murray. That's what takes away my worries."

"Oh, I love to dance!"

"Well, you should come to one of our dances. We have one this Wednesday. You can be my guest."

"Let's see," she said, and looked at her phone as though checking her schedule. "Well, I'm not sure right now. What's your phone number?"

That should have triggered a qualm or two, but I was thinking dancing, so I gave her my number.

"Okay," I said, "let me know and I'll give you the address."

After we had both returned to our workouts, I felt that it had been a rather nice encounter. It's not every day an attractive young woman I've never met engages me in such an enthusiastic manner. The young women working out here mostly ignore me. I notice them, but regard them as I would my granddaughters.

But no big deal. I figured that Esther is most likely just another nice gal like Denise, who addressed me one day, complimenting me for working out.

But a couple of days later, on Thursday, I was in the stretching area, and little Esther appeared suddenly, and started a conversation like we were old friends.

"Hi Barney, I'm sorry I couldn't make it to the dance, I was helping a friend that night."

"Oh, that's okay."

"So, um," she said, "Will you be here on Sunday? I really want to see you then."

"Well, no, I don't come here on Sundays."

"Oh, but this is so important! It's at 7:00 p.m. and it's a . . . spiritual session. It's hard to explain, but the more people that come, the more successful it will be."

I wondered if it was some kind of healing ceremony, for her cancer. "Why is it so important that I be there?"

"Because, you are so . . . special. I knew it from the first." She looked at me with a sweet smile that I imagine was supposed to be seductive.

"But you just met me how do you know I'm special?"

"I know it's hard to understand . . . but I just know!"

Flattering, but it doesn't make sense. I explained that Sunday evening my son comes over, and then I eat at 7:00.

"Oh, but please come!" she pleaded. "Look, you were in the military, and you know how sometimes you have to drop everything and go help a friend who needs you? That's what this is like."

"Well, I'll see what I can do, but I can't promise."

Sunday evening at 6:30 p.m., my son Will was here listening to my description of Esther's enigmatic request. Then my phone rang. "I bet it's her," I said as I put the phone to my ear.

"Hello, Barney, how are you?" she purred.

"Is this . . . Esther?"

"Yes."

"Well I'm fine, but I have to tell you that I can't come over tonight. But you said the session was spiritual, so how about if I'm just there in spirit. At exactly seven o'clock I'll meditate, think only of you, and send some good, healing vibes, okay?"

"Well . . . okay, that would be nice."

At 7:00 p.m., I actually sat and meditated, sending good thoughts to Esther. Did I really think this would work?

I didn't see her for a few days. Then one day, as I was just leaving the gym, she materialized in front of me. "Did you get my message?" she asked. "I texted you to tell you that your thoughts came through to me last Sunday."

"Well, that's wonderful, but I didn't get your message because my phone is a dumb old flip phone that doesn't take texts."

— ◇ —

Many weeks passed and I figured I'd never see her again. But I was still curious as to what of bizarre game she was playing.

Then one day at lunchtime in the dining room, I got a call from Esther. She sounded very distraught and confused. "I need to talk to you," she sobbed, "I need help!" Her voice broke and she seemed panic stricken. I told her that if she could come over here where I live, I would meet her out front. She said that was impossible, as it was "dangerous" for her to come to this part of town. She added that she couldn't come to the gym or even her own apartment right by the gym.

"Where are you staying?" I asked.

"In my car, and sometimes a motel . . . do you have a car?" she asked, crying desperately. "Can you come over here to me?"

I explained that I didn't drive because I was legally blind. She gasped in surprise and disappointment. I felt so sorry for her. By this time, I felt sure that she had a mental illness.

"Oh, I don't know what I'll do," she cried, "I just feel awful and no one here will help me!" Her voice wavered with emotion.

So once again I resorted to the spiritual rescue. "I'll meditate," I told her, "and send you my most positive thoughts. Be open for them at exactly six o'clock tonight. I'm hoping that will help you." I suggested that she call me the following day to let me know how she's doing.

At noon the next day she called, and she sounded like a different person. "It worked! I got back on my meds, and now I'm at my new gym and met some friends, and I'm so much better!"

I was so pleased to hear her joy and relief. But who knows how long it would last, for example, if she was bipolar.

I will probably never know. Nor can I be sure that I have any psychic powers, or if it was all in her head. At any rate, if I helped her, that's all that matters.

Two years have now passed, and I'm in the gym, still doing my thing. As I enter the TRX workout room, I notice an attractive young lady as I pass by. Attractive women is not unusual for this place. But then she comes over to me. "Hi, it's so good to see you here!"

Déjà vu?? No. I recognize her then. She is the physical therapist that worked with me for my sore hip. After a couple of words, we continued our workouts.

There will never be another Esther. I just hope the girl is well and happy.

CHAPTER 23
SHOWCASE!

DANCE EXTRAVAGANZA!

SEPTEMBER 11, 2021

"Another Showcase?" I said to my dance teacher, Wren, as she handed me a pamphlet. I had gone to only one Showcase before. And it was clear across the seas in London. An adventure, for sure.

[You can read about my London Showcase caper in my book, *Dancing with Arthritis at Arthur Murray—Why I started dance lessons at age 86.*]

A Showcase is a big deal and I hadn't considered doing another one. But this one was near Lake Tahoe, only a couple of hours drive, in Truckee, where I used to love to live!

The brochure named the specific location as the Ritz-Carlton Hotel. I didn't know they had such a high end hotel in my little Truckee. Then I remembered. The Ritz is actually at Northstar, the ski resort. It had disgusted me that a fancy-dancy hotel for rich people was going to be in my little unpretentious mountain town.

Nevertheless, I was intrigued by the concept of taking part in such a prestigious event that was to happen in my old stompin' ground. The pamphlet offered several different packages. One was called *Master of the Spear.* "Wow, if I chose this one I'd have to do forty dances!"

That's not so many," Wren says. "With *Master of the sword* you'd have to do eighty." Well, forget the sword guy.

So I chose the *cheapest* package. But cheap is a misnomer, because none of this was *cheap.*

But now I was committed. I reasoned that it would be a good way to force me to upgrade my dancing skills. It would take tons of practice so I took even more out of my savings and doubled my dance lessons. Fortunately, I had recently acquired an extra pile of cash from the profit of my above mentioned book about dancing. (The CEO of Arthur Murray International had liked my book so much that he bought 300 copies from me.)

Then Wren dropped the bombshell: She was not going to be at this Showcase Dance.

I would be practicing with other instructors.

Aye! Old people hate change! I'd been with Wren for over two years, through thick and thin, pre-pandemic and even virtual lessons during the lockdown. She knew my strengths and weaknesses. I was familiar with her teaching style.

Although I wasn't happy with this unexpected development, I put on a London "stiff upper lip" and went along with it. The other teachers were good and I figured that it probably would be good for me to get used to other teachers.

But other obstacles kept mounting. After weeks of freedom from COVID masks, we were told masks were to be mandated again. *Holy cow! Forty dances wearing a mask?* And the wildfires in the Sierra were raging, with smoke pouring into Truckee.

Finally, after weeks of trying to accustom myself to two different teaching styles, I felt unprepared, frustrated and discouraged. I wanted out.

I told Gerard, the Arthur Murray Folsom business manager, that I wanted to withdraw from the Showcase. He was shocked. But Gerard is a very astute and innovative person.

"Oh, no, you don't have to do that! We'll work something out." He was so positive.

And then he made me the proverbial *offer I couldn't refuse.* "Ronit (pronounced ro-neet) is back to teach full time," he enthused. "She has agreed to take over." Ronnie was a married lady with adult children, but her figure and grace was envied by twenty-year-old girls. I had enjoyed this vivacious and charming lady as my teacher two years prior. This was a golden solution.

However, we only had two more practice sessions left before the gala event. Would it be enough? Would I screw up my dance moves, make a fool of myself, be an embarrassment for Arthur Murray Folsom?

Then I mentally kicked myself off of that crappy pile of angst. What the hell? This is what I've been promising myself! *Keep moving. Get out of your comfort zone. At age ninety-two this will be your Shasta climb, your Tahoe Half Marathon! Go for it!*

We arrived at my beloved Tahoe domain Friday afternoon, September 10, 2021. The sun beamed down from the gorgeous blue sky through clean air. My driver and companion, Lori, and I walked into the highfalutin' hotel that I had sworn I would never grace with my presence.

I was lucky that Lori, one of my fellow dancers, had agreed to provide our transportation. Lori is a cute, gracious lady, and would prove to be extremely helpful over the weekend, guiding "Mr. Magoo" around the vast interior of the edifice.

We checked in, declining the free glass of champagne, and went to find our rooms. I was disoriented as we walked a quarter mile down the hallway, until I came to room 337; I couldn't see which way to put the key card in, so Lori showed me.

I stepped in and scanned the interior of my two-night abode. *Wow!* I thought. *Conspicuous opulence. King bed, minibar, white robes in the closet. I'm not used to so much ritziness. I don't need it. But—I'll let myself indulge in it for now. What the heck, once in a lifetime!*

That evening, Lori and I got together with fellow dancers Robert and Naomi for dinner.

It was a lovely evening with lovely people.

The next morning, I rushed up to Ronit in a panic. "I forgot the steps for the *Junior Walk* in the Foxtrot," I gasped. So we tried it, and it came right back to me. Sigh of relief.

Then the dancing began. First came the *smooth dances:* waltz, fox trot and tango. I did them all. After the first two dances, I relaxed and decided to just have fun, mistakes be damned! Nobody's perfect.

After the smooth dances, we moved on to the rhythm segment: rhumba, salsa, cha cha, swing, hustle, and Lindy hop.

Ronit babysat me the whole day because I couldn't read the dance program. She would say, "Okay, after two dances, we go on again for an east coast swing, then a rhumba and a cha cha. Then you can rest for five dances and then we have the Hustle and another Lindy, back to back."

The Lindy hop is an exuberant dance, with a backrock (rock back with one foot) then two energetic kicks forward. I heard the MC, Bobby, from our own Arthur Murray Folsom, announce at the end on one of my Lindys, "Yep, and he's ninety-two, folks."

At another time, Bobby plugged my aforementioned book about dancing: ". . . and the Arthur Murray president liked it so much," he said, "that he bought enough to distribute to all the

Arthur Murray centers." Ronit and I had stayed on the dance floor after the music stopped, so I waved to the crowd, acknowledging that I was the author.

Occasionally throughout the afternoon, someone would ask, "Are you the one who wrote that book?" One lady approached and declared proudly, "I dance with arthritis too!" After which a nice conversation ensued. At 4:00 p.m. I was about to do my last dance. Bobby's voice rang out, "Hey, everybody, this is Harvey's last dance." I was hoping they wouldn't watch me too closely, because by then I was pooped, not in my best form.

Ronit had not only kept me on schedule, but also made sure I had drinks and snacks, and had time to go to the bathroom. She was my angel!

Later, after a shower and rest, decked out in suit and bolo tie, I followed Lori down for the cocktail hour. My one beer cost thirteen dollars. I gave them fifteen and said, "Keep the change." Like a big shot. What the heck, might as well play along.

Dinner that night was a formal, four-course affair, with place cards, a different fork for each course, and wine for those who desired it.

Soon, the professional show started, with all the dance teachers, and choreographed by Wesley from our Folsom studio.

It was magnificent! A love story, and our very own Claire was the star. It was so superb that I felt like I was at a New York Broadway production.

I had felt considerable anxiety and doubt as to whether I should have made this plunge into the *big time.* I'm so thankful I didn't miss this adventure.

I owe a lot to the Arthur Murray Folsom staff and students for the magnanimous support I got that day. Dancing has become part of my being. As long as my legs and feet function, I will be involved in this magic realm.

CHAPTER 24
SPOTLIGHT ARTHUR MURRAY FOLSOM

NOVEMBER 6, 2021

The Tahoe dance extravaganza in September boosted my confidence. I was ready for more.

That chance came soon, for on November 6, our very own studio put on a Spotlight right here in Folsom. This time, however, I bravely decided to do a solo: Just my teacher and me, performing before the multitudes as they scrutinized our dance prowess.

The typical solo routine is one dance style practiced to perfection. But since I'm not perfect, I wanted our solo to be ... unconventional. We therefore inserted several elements into our routine to fulfill this aspiration: 1-The song itself was tongue-in-cheek, about a guy that had been dumped, and went to great measures to win her back. This poor dude was a mess, so, in desperation, he started dance lessons to impress her.

Ronit and I played the roles of that boy and girl.

2-We did five different dance styles, including one that I made up myself, called *the Barney Bee Bop*

3-We programmed two times during the middle of the performance for the music to abruptly stop for a few seconds, during which we both froze in place. This fooled the spectators, who began their applause, but after five seconds, the music and dancing came alive with a start.

To get ready for this I had to practice at home with the same soundtrack. Getting the timing right was important and difficult.

The song begins with the jilted guy lamenting his woes: "You're tearing my heart to bits!" I pull my hands apart violently, as though my heart is breaking in two.

"You told me to go get lost." I slump, head down, and turn away.

Meanwhile, Ronit, playing the girl who had spurned me, is a few feet away, ignoring me.

"But hey, girl," the song lyrics continue, "you ran me off, but here I am!"

I pivot rapidly, to face Ronit.

This gets the girl's attention, and she turns toward me with a gesture like, *Are you talking to me?*

I stand as tall as I can. "Check this out, young lady!" The music comes on loud with a fast rock-and-roll number and I launch into a fast Barney Bee Bop. Ronit fans herself with excitement. Then I change to a jitterbug. She looks delighted and starts sauntering eagerly toward me as I change to a vigorous *single time swing.* We meet, do a couple of two-hand turns, then with one hand I spin her twice.

The song lyrics ring out with "Look at what I can do!" We initiate a peppy Lindy hop. Then I change to a solo Mashed Potatoes, and Ronit steps up beside me and copies me, then I take her hands and we start jitterbugging.

Then the music stops abruptly, as we scored it, and we freeze, slightly crouched, face to face. Applause, interrupted by music and more jitterbugging. Then another music freeze, applause, interrupted by music for our Barney Bee Bop, and finish with a sudden but graceful dip.

A roaring applause erupts, uninterrupted this time, and best of all, I hear a lot of laughing. It feels good to make people happy.

Chapter 25
Losing Belly Fat

MARCH 2022

Losing belly fat may not sound like an adventure. And I do admit that, compared to the abundance of zealous exhilaration I experienced while skiing Shasta and the Teton Range, doing battle with a bigger than desired jelly roll sounds pretty weak. (Do you suppose this nosedive in the degree of physical challenge and risk could be age related?) However, it may surprise you how much adventure I can milk out of old cows like Bean Bags and Belly Fat.

When I mentioned to one of my friends here in *The Home* that I was trying to get rid of my belly blubber, they thought I was overreacting. "Oh, come off it, Harvey," Dora exclaimed, "you don't have a big belly!"

Well, thanks for the reassurance, friend, but tell that to my belt which I have to keep expanding!

I had never had this problem before. When I was eighty, my stomach was flat and one of my doctors said I was underweight. Then I had to move back down to the flatlands, and that ended my mountaineering escapades.

So, I started working out at the gym, but in spite of that exercise, my belly metamorphosed gradually from flat to what resembled an early stage of pregnancy. But my contemporaries shrugged it off, telling me, "Our bodies change as we get older, get used to it!"

Well, I couldn't muster up much enthusiasm for the old-age excuse, so I sought counsel from a friend of mine who was a fitness expert. "If you do the same thing with every workout" she said, "your muscles just yawn and say, 'hey, same old thing, no challenge here!'"

Okay, desperate times, desperate measures. So I hired a trainer at the fitness center named Daniel, and I outlined my goals to him:

1. Reduce belly fat.2. Vary my workouts. 3. Fine tune my nutritional intake.

Daniel perused my personal diet, and said it didn't need to be tweaked much, but I had to incorporate different activities in my workouts, as well as extending their length. So he started me on an impressive array of new exercises that had funny names. The one called *TRX single leg speed tube* is good for both strength and balance. Then there's the *stagger step twist,* which makes me feel like I'm doing a cool martial arts move.

Then there are the beloved squats, like the TRX wide squats, and, not to be left out, the narrow squat as well. And don't forget the frontal squats at the rail by machine #183. *Ooh, that didn't feel good on my hamstring.*

Ah, but these are but a dearth of all the new moves, as well as the usual machines, like leg extension and chest press. Suffice it to say, I had an abundance of fitness moves to keep my muscles and fibers from getting bored.

And, besides walking the mile to the gym, I also started walking home as well, instead of wimping out and taking the bus back. Freedom from deadlines of the city bus schedules was nice, so I could stay longer. I actually enjoyed the walks, and sang songs or recited poetry as I ambled along.

It was going well. Besides upgrading my workouts, I doubled my dance lessons on Fridays, and went to the dance parties Wednesday nights. More importantly, my pants were starting to fit. This was starting to work. Life is good.

But . . . something was gnawing at my sense of well being. My hamstring had been quietly trying to get my attention. Then it raised its voice until it was shouting. It started to bother me on my walks and some exercises. I could ignore it no longer. My right leg was golden, but by comparison, my left limb was a rusty, crumpled mess of tin foil.

On April 5th, 2022, my doctor said, "you have to give it two weeks absolute rest." UGH! No dancing, or walking, no workouts. No life.

Then I started physical therapy. My athletic doctor friend, Blair, advised me: "It will probably take at least five or six weeks of therapy to see a difference."

I hoped I could do better than that. I began the therapy in mid-April, and saw that I was scheduled through June. *Would it really take that long?* My therapist, Matt, told me, "The longer you've had it, the longer it takes to heal." I had had it off and on for two years.

But Matt was very thorough, and I felt confident he knew what he was doing. He himself had also experienced a hamstring injury. Matt was determined to heal me, and so was I.

He prescribed a regimen of four hundred and twenty stretches to do daily. Actually it was only thirteen, but it seemed like more because I was already doing stretches for my Achilles tendon, and now I had thirteen more.

Some days after therapy, I was more sore than before. I learned then that proper treatment includes strengthening the connecting muscles, and even though it did smart a bit, this is what Matt was accomplishing when he had me push against resistance. Any pain soon went away, and the muscles were stronger.

Then my arthritic hips flared up. Again, that was because I was no longer doing any aerobic exercise or walking. The best medicine for arthritis is *movement.* *"Movement is medicine and motion is lotion."* So then I incorporated hip stretches into my regimen.

But I was antsy to get moving again, so I asked Matt, "Can I start taking walks?"

"Just ten minutes, max," he insisted. "Five minutes out, and five minutes back." *Okay, not much, but better than a jab in the eye with a sharp stick.*

The following week I really pressed my luck. "How 'bout if I got a ride to the gym and only worked out the upper body?" Matt surprised me with an affirmative answer. "But you still have to do the daily stretches I gave you."

Okay, I was *back at the gym!*

The elliptical and StairMaster were off limits , but at least I could do the chest presses, rail push up and other upper body stuff.

After four weeks of Matt's aggressive therapy, and all the assigned at-home stretches, I could detect only a slight smidgen of improvement. They say that "Any long journey starts with a small step." But how long was this journey going to be?

But I kept plodding, stretching and pushing through minor pain maneuvers. And the symptoms slowly lessened. I graduated from two physical therapy sessions a week to just one.

Then Matt introduced me to the *Monster Walk.* I guess it's common therapy, but I thought it was a real kick-in-the-butt funny exercise. Shackled by a flexible band around my ankles, knees slightly bent in a mini-squat, I was supposed to walk, taking slow big steps. I felt so much like a real monster that I decided I had to growl and roar menacingly. So I tried to terrorize Pauline, the only young damsel around, an assistant. But that didn't work out, because it just made her laugh.

Then Matt increased my homework to fourteen moves daily. This was getting more fun all the time!

This hamstring layoff would be the longest span of inactivity since my heart bypass surgery in 2003. I hadn't been walking or dancing much, and my ankles became slightly swollen. "Most likely," my doc said, "because you're less active, so the blood doesn't circulate as well." *More collateral damage! And my pants are getting as tight as before!*

But I had no choice, because the hamstring was still tender. On May 27, I tripped and came down hard on my bad left leg to keep from falling. This re-injured it and set me back three weeks.

But when the weather warmed up in June and July, I started swimming. With my weak flutter kick, no problem. But in my swimming suit, my belly looked ever bigger to me.

As July wore on, I started working on the elliptical, a machine for walking with handles for arm movements as well. I started going on longer walks, gradually increasing the distance.

Then I was exposed to COVID, so was quarantined for a few days. But I still snuck out for a few solo walks.

Back at the gym I sampled the StairMaster and slowly increased my elliptical time. And I kept up all my homework stretches and strengthening. Not just the bad leg, but both of them, so I wouldn't be walking in circles when I was recovered.

Finally, on July 23, I started up my dance lessons again, carefully. No Lindy hop or polkas yet! And the following week at Lake Tahoe with family, I did a three and a half mile hike with my son Brian. That was a good test, as it involved some climbing. The hamstring wasn't sore, but I iced it anyway after each outing.

On August 5, after a three week hiatus, I returned to my therapist. He performed a thorough evaluation. The results were so favorable that he released me, reminding me to keep up my treatments at home. Good news!

I knew my hamstring wasn't totally healed, but figured I could do most of my activities. But the night that my dance studio helped me celebrate my ninety-third birthday, I danced the polka and the Lindy hop for the first time in months. It was fun and felt fine.

Until the following day! Then the stubborn hamstring growled and moaned, giving me notice that just those two dances were off limits for quite a long time yet.

But eventually, it seemed to be totally healed. I've upgraded my workouts and doubled my dance lessons. I'm once again going to the evening dance parties. My routines are getting back to normal. Life is good.

Now—if I can just start losing some of this belly fat.

CHAPTER 26

SNORKELING IN MEXICO

"Belly Fat" was going to be my last chapter until another adventure unexpectedly sprang into my life.

During conversations with my sons Will and Brian, I had remarked, "Gee, the snorkeling sounds fun. I've done a lot of things, but I've never gone snorkeling."

The regret must have shown on my face, because my family took this remark and ran with it. The snorkeling seed germinated with Tresa and Will, and spread to Brian and Lance. And through the months the plans for the great excursion evolved.

"This is a trip we're planning for you, Dad," Will informed me. "So you can go snorkeling."

Incredible! A family excursion tailored especially for this old curmudgeon. But since I was a total snorkel-virgin, I found myself in Will's back yard pool in September of 2022 wearing a snorkeling mask. My kids' idea—so I could get some practice.

I kept inserting the breathing apparatus incorrectly. The thought of keeping my face in the water to breathe intimidated me. But finally I clamped down on the mouthpiece, put my head down and sucked in air! I was snorkeling!

"That's good, Dad!" Will said, "but now you have to learn how to clear it."

"What do you mean?"

"Get the water out of the tube."

"I thought that's what the snorkel was for."

"Yeah, but in the ocean sometimes the waves will get water in the system, and you have to blow it out." He demonstrated how to do it: PUUHFF! It was a quick, sharp exhalation. "Kind of like a cough," Will said. He had me dive to get water in the tube, and then clear it. I think I did it, because the water spurted out. During this time Will had his phone out so that Brian could watch on FaceTime. Will told me that Brian had suggested that Will do a *cannon ball* right beside me to make it seem like an ocean wave. When I got home I practiced just the PUUHFF-ing part. Got that much down pat anyway.

Through the following months, my intrepid family made the travel and lodging reservations. The location would be La Paz, down on the southern tip of Baja California at a nice resort. The accommodations sounded great. I would have my own room and private bathroom, because I am like a special needs kid who has gotten old. Everything was arranged and final. We were all excited!

But my excitement felt dulled when my swollen ankles worsened. I had suddenly gained six pounds of water weight. At the Wednesday night dance at my Arthur Murray center, I got so exhausted that I had to stop in the middle of a salsa dance.

The next day my doctor's office called to let me know that the X-ray showed that water had infiltrated my lungs and heart. I was afflicted with congestive heart failure.

My doctor prescribed five new medications, each with side effects. I felt spaced out and exhausted half the time.

But worse was ponderous question that weighed on all our minds: *Would I still be able to go on our wonderful Mexican excursion?*

Dragging myself out of bed at 2:45 a.m. was hard, but I didn't care. I got my doctor's clearance and I was going with my family to Mexico! This dark morning was Tuesday, April eighteenth, 2023, the day we had all anticipated for months.

I traveled with Will, his wife, Tresa, and their twenty-one-year-old daughter Mimi. We would meet their other daughter Amelia and her boyfriend Randy when they boarded at Los Angeles where we changed planes. The plan then was to meet Brian, Lance and the fourteen-year-old twins, Kylah and Tegan at Cabo San Lucas, Mexico.

The dreaded air travel with layovers was sweetened somewhat by the snazzy lounges we had the privilege of using with cushy couches and free food and drink. All Will and Tresa had to do to get us all in was show the doorkeepers their phones. They must have something magic in them. It pays to travel with high class people.

After the final reunion in Cabo, we all piled in the van with driver Octavio and after about two hours and a lunch stop, arrived at La Paz. To get to our lodging, we hopped on the water taxi for the seven minute ride. On the way, we were delighted by the company of some dolphins jumping and swimming beside our boat. We didn't know that this would be just to preview of several other dolphin encounters.

The resort, called *Paraiso del Mar* (Paradise of the Sea), was technically on a peninsula, but it seemed like an island to me. Our accommodations were comprised of apartment-like complexes with several bedrooms, full kitchen, living area and verandas.

I stayed in Brian's complex and Will and family were in another building next door. My room was spacious with a large bathroom. My veranda looked out onto a gorgeous view of countless palm trees, green landscaping, the big blue swimming pool with the Gulf of California in the background.

The first couple of days, we settled in, went grocery shopping, and I did some more snorkel practice in the cozy warm pool.

Thursday night we dined out at the golf club restaurant, said to be the best on the island. All ten of us walked in there at seven p.m. with good appetites. Two hours later they finally started to bring us our food.

But there was live entertainment in the interim: a raccoon—very comfortable in its domicile, hangin' out in the rafters above us. He had time to do several encores before our hunger was assuaged. I imagined that the little critter was bemused by these out-of-towners, and most likely felt superior as he looked down on us foreign intruders. I was just hoping he wasn't right above our table when we finally had plates of food.

The next morning, Friday, we hustled ourselves to the dock and boarded the boat that would take us to an archipelago by the name of *Espiritu Santo*. (Holy Spirit), in the Gulf of California.

Our craft was a skiff, open air, rather small, but big enough to carry our ten family members, a crew of two, plus our eco-friendly and knowledgeable guide, Miguel.

The islands we were approaching are of volcanic origin. This island complex, 25 kilometers from the city of La Paz, was given the honorific title *Patrimonia de la Humanidad* (World Heritage) in 2005. Then in 2007 its status was elevated to a national park, thanks to the great abundance of biodiversity, which makes this area unique.

For example, Miguel pointed out a blue-footed booby, a bird we had thought was confined to the Galapagos Islands.

On one island we caught sight of a high, white ridge as we passed. "What is all that white?" Brian asked. "Salt?"

"No," Miguel answered, "it's all bird droppings."

Wow, that's one impressive pile of avian poop!

"And when it rains," Miguel continued, "it is washed into the sea."

Bummer—pollution.

But Miguel clarified that it was a good thing, because the droppings serve as food for the coral reefs in these waters.

Good ol' Mother Nature, working her miracles!

Then Miguel, slowing his speech down, announce that we were coming to a small island called La Lobera. "Home," he said with a tinge of pride, "of one of the largest reproductive colonies of *lobos marinos* (sea wolves) in the world. (They are what we call sea lions.)

And we'd be swimming with Miguel's "charismatic animals," because this was to be the venue for our snorkeling exploit.

Wow! This was the big moment—the whole reason for putting this expedition together—to give grandpa a chance to snorkel! I slipped smoothly into the clear, tepid water. It felt heavenly. I floated effortlessly as beheld some exotic, multi-colored fish and some mollusks. And was that a coral reef down there?

No, not really. That's just what you expected to read. *Yawn.* All nice and good, but this Jones clan is also open to adventure peppered with a dash of the atypical.

Here's how it really went down: I plunged awkwardly off of the boat, scraping my arm. When I hit the water, the cold took my breath away. (I think the temperature was about 71°.) We all wore wet suits, but me, who used to go skiing in blizzards had become acutely sensitive to cold. I quickly bit down on the mouthpiece, breathing and moving. Brian was on one side of me and Will on the other, holding my hand for reassurance. I was a bit dismayed that I couldn't see anything in this depth. But soon it was shallow enough to see much more. We were getting close to the wolves. One swam right by me. I wanted to stay and see more, but I could tell my wimpy old body couldn't endure the low temperature any longer. Miguel got me back to the boat, and a crew member bandaged my bleeding arm.

I was glad the others were still enjoying snorkeling. When Tresa came in, she said, "I touched one of them!" When Brian and Will came in they told me, "You did it, Dad!" Yes, I did. Despite the brevity of my first snorkeling in the choppy high seas, I felt good about it.

Next on the tour was the clean sandy beach where they served us a nice lunch. Here we could lay back in the warmth of the sun and tranquility. A few went snorkeling again. I got so comfortable, reclined on a blanket, that I dozed off for a while.

Our return trip back to the resort was more direct, but enhanced by the sightings of several different schools of dolphins as we sailed along. They frolicked and splashed playfully, even sidling up to our boat at times.

Our guide, Miguel, asked, "Do you want to see me swim with the dolphins?" He dived in and disappeared, then we saw him with the dolphins. He seemed to be keeping up with their pace. Miguel is obviously comfortable in his natural marine world.

Pelicans and frigates kept circling over concentrations of hungry dolphins who were driving fish closer to the surface to corral them for dinner.

That also made it easier for the birds to get a quick lunch.

—◇—

Back on land, I felt inspired enough by the day's events that I broke out in a popular Mexican folk song, *Cielito Lindo: "Aye, aye aye aye, canta and no llores."*

Although this day had been the highlight, we also enjoyed spending time at the pool, dining out, walking along the *Malecón*, (A popular main drag along the waterfront), and just hanging out with family we hadn't seen for a while.

On the last day I got to ride along with twins, Kylah and Tegan, as they learned how to drive golf carts.

The trip back home was uneventful except for a minor row we almost caused. We used my blindness as a way for Will and me to board our flight first, so that this water-pill-pappy could be assured of a seat close to the restroom. *We'll go to the very back and save some seats.* But masses swarmed to the back, clamoring for the vacant spots.

"Oh, no!" the flight attendant protested to Will, "you can't save seats."

"But they're coming," Will countered, "I see them."

"No, there are people right here who need a seat. Are you going to be a problem?"

"No, I won't be a problem," Will said with a grin, as he vacated the row in front of me and came back beside me, still holding one seat for Tresa.

As always, it's good to be home. I was looking forward to a Spotlight Dance at my Arthur Murray studio the following Saturday. But I will treasure the memories of this family adventure forever.

Epilogue

Today, is it is now August 18,2023.

I am so grateful for the blessed life I've been lucky enough to lead. But looking ahead I feel a heavy weight of angst because of global warming and the reluctance by some entities, such as the fossil feel industries, to reduce carbon emissions.

I want my young descendants to have a good quality of life, like I have had. I wish I could donate the rest of my years in exchange for their happiness— a very small sacrifice on my part.

So instead, I'll do what little I can about climate change and nurse an optimism that mankind will finally do what is necessary to ensure a good future for these younger generations that we leave behind.

And you, the younger set, will have to prepare yourselves, be activist and do what you can to protect yourselves and the planet. But I hope my generation has by then shucked off their denial and apathy and acted to reverse the trend.

I love all my family dearly, but you younger ones are especially in my heart as I write this in the dusk of my life.

H.B. (Grandpa) Jones

Author's Note

MY ADVENTURES IN OTHER BOOKS

From *True Tales of a Wyoming Generation* by H. Barnett Jones:

"Jumping, Flying, and Floating for 65" (chapter 46)
- Sky diving

"Summer Travels" (chapter 48)
- Hut-to-hut hiking in Spain and Norway
- Circumambulating Mt. Blanc in France, Italy and Switzerland
- Hiking the Inca Trail to Machu Picchu
- Cycling along the Loire River in France
- Monitoring an active volcano in Costa Rica

From *True Tales Slightly Skewed* by H. Barnett Jones:

"Lost at Mount Shasta" (chapter 8)
"White Water Paranoia" (chapter 9)
- Rafting the Colorado river in the Grand Canyon.

Made in the USA
Columbia, SC
06 September 2023